Create Your Own
Family Record
A Gift for the Future

Create Your Own
Family Record

A Gift for the Future

EILEEN PECK

ARCTURUS

Published by Arcturus Publishing Limited
For Bookmart Limited
Registered number 2372865
Trading as Bookmart Limited
Desford Road, Enderby, Leicester LE9 5AD

This edition published 2002

© Arcturus Publishing Limited
1-7 Shand Street, London SE1 2ES

ISBN 1-84193-118-7

Printed in Denmark by Norhaven Paperbacks, Viborg

Author: Eileen Peck
Illustrator: Jim Hansen
Editor: Rebecca Panayiotou
Text Designer: Zeta Fitzpatrick @ Moo
Cover Designer: Alex Ingr

CONTENTS

INTRODUCTION

This book is the result of years of my wondering just what my great-grandparents were like... and their parents... and their parents. I'm lucky in that I have lots of family photographs going back two generations into the last years of the 19th century. Studying these pictures I can see family likenesses - the tall stature, the wide-set eyes, the shape of the face.

But when I wonder what my forebears, including great aunts and uncles, were like, my thoughts go beyond physical appearance to their personalities and the world in which they were living. How did they spend their time? What was happening in the world during their lifetimes? How did they make sense of their lives? What preoccupations did they have? What made them happy - and sad?

My interest in past family members stems from the realisation that I know so very little about them. If I was interested in the life of say, Abraham Lincoln or Henry VIII, I could find out far more about them than I could ever know about my own great-grandmother. Although she died less than 100 years ago, the facts of her life are lost forever. This is a sadness to me.

I can remember just two occasions when sudden, brief glimpses into the past have filled me with excitement. My husband found a cassette recording he had made of his father, just a year before the old man died. With some prompting from my husband, his father was reminiscing about his life - jobs he had done and people he had known. It was the very sound of his voice, as well as his little jokes about people he knew, that brought him briefly back to life.

Even more thrilling was when I found an old letter as I was helping to clear out my mother's attic after she had died. The letter fell out of a pile of magazines and was sent by her father to her mother during the First World War. I was already familiar with the posed studio portrait of my grandfather in his uniform, with a small cameo of my grandmother, mother and aunt superimposed high up in the corner. This was a common practice among photographers at the time and the idea was, I suppose, to signify that they were in his thoughts. The letter was loving and was obviously designed to reassure my grandmother that all was well at the Front. I felt privileged to have glimpsed something of their relationship. What's more, the handwriting was very similar to my mother's - a real link with the past. It also occurred to me that I was very lucky to find the letter, and that I would now store it with the photograph.

The little we know of our past family is likely to have come to us in one of two ways. Either something, most likely some photographs, has come into our possession almost by chance, or it could be that we or another family member has researched our family history. The shelves in public libraries and bookshops are bulging with books about 'How to Trace your Family Tree'. Researching family history has become a popular hobby. If we are so interested in our own past, we can assume that future generations will be interested in us.

I'm not suggesting that it is necessary to spend hours researching your family history, or to take on the daunting task of writing an autobiography, although these are tasks you might decide you would like to take on. No, the task can be more fun and far less time-consuming. The guidelines in this book describe simple ways in which you can preserve aspects of your life and the world in which you live without necessarily spending a lot of time or effort. By following these suggestions you can communicate something of yourself to future generations so that they won't have to rely on the unlikely chance of finding the odd letter or unlabelled photograph.

Without doubt, anything that is presented in a way which is compact, durable and easy for future generations to store will become a valuable family heirloom. By spending just a few hours now you can help future generations to understand something of their family background and of how they became who they are. In our rapidly changing world such knowledge will help to give them the security that comes from knowing where you fit in, where you stand in the world. You could consider the contribution you are making as a 'Gift for the Future'.

The Gift will be all the more valuable if you use materials that are long-lasting and if you keep it in favourable conditions. Guidelines on this are given towards the end of the book.

If you are not yet using the Internet you might be a bit daunted by my suggestion that you use it for various aspects of your Gift. Please don't worry about this - just look on it as a challenge which, if you take it on, will be very rewarding. If you don't have access to the Internet at home try your local library - many offer beginners courses - or an Internet café, where you could just go and dabble. If you don't want to use the Internet that's fine, but if you can overcome any initial reticence you will be surprised at the information you can find simply at the touch of a button.

If you feel unsure about embarking on the project, be reassured by the fact that everyone who was asked to write a short piece about their lives as a contribution to this book did so very willingly. Not only that, but they all said that they found the experience very enjoyable, thought-provoking and, in some cases, moving.

I hope that pondering on and recording your life so far will be a positive experience. Even if you do not show your completed 'package' to anyone, by the very creation of it you will be affirming yourself in a positive way which will be helpful to you now and in the future. We have all made mistakes and most of us have some regrets, but I hope that by working on your Gift you will be able to throw the spotlight onto your achievements, however small. The experience of producing our own individual Gift will be different for each of us. Whether you complete it in a weekend or a year, the result will be something to be valued for generations to come. It might also lead you to re-evaluate your life and perhaps change your direction. Or it might simply help you to value and enjoy who you are and the life that you have.

Eileen Peck

PART I

GETTING STARTED

YOU DON'T NEED TO BE A WRITER - BE CREATIVE!

The starting point for thinking about your life and times and how to record something of them is to cast from your mind the idea that it will all be too time-consuming and difficult. Nothing could be further from the truth. You don't need to devote months or years of your life to the project. By being creative and working through these guidelines on the basis of pick 'n' mix you will be able to produce, in a very short time, a 'Gift for the Future' which preserves the essence of yourself and your life and times.

Next, forget about the word 'autobiography' which might well conjure up pictures of the rich and famous. You might not be rich

and famous but be assured that your life and times are unique and interesting. While writing may well be the basic tool for many people preserving their Life Story, if you find it difficult or too time-consuming then this can be kept to a minimum.

Writing is indeed a very effective means of communicating, but it is by no means the only way. There are plenty of examples of other very effective means of communicating:

The Arts

We all know that artists communicate through their work, in fact, it is often said that art forms - say, a painting or piece of music - can communicate what is impossible to put into words. Just think of how music can bring tears to your eyes or can help raise your spirits and make you smile. The communication here is pretty powerful.

Clothing

People communicate a great deal about themselves by what they wear - in fact clothes are an essential part of the face an individual presents to the world, a means by which he can express his identity. Teenagers 'wouldn't be seen dead' in certain items of clothing that would be their parents' choice, but prefer to wear something which communicates that they are part of a certain group. Young people often shun the idea of wearing a school uniform yet, when given a choice in what they would like to wear, dress alike and look remarkably 'uniform', just to communicate to the world that they belong together, are in the same gang.

Photography

You might have a favourite photograph of say, a family holiday which captures in one moment what the holiday was about. Pictures can say so much. Two people are asked for a photograph of themselves enjoying what they consider to be their very favourite day. One produces a picture of a country scene where they are climbing over a stile, while the other shows a picture of themselves with their family at Disney World. It could be deduced that one enjoyed the peace and quiet of the countryside while the other relished the excitement, noise and bustle of theme parks and fun-fair rides. You can say so much with a single picture. If carefully chosen, it can say far more than an album full of formally posed portraits.

Music

Three people might be asked to name their favourite piece of music. One says he enjoys a loud and dramatic piece by Wagner while a second enjoys jazz and a third chooses something by the

Sex Pistols or Madonna. The choice of music says something about an individual's personality.

It has also been suggested that the instrument which a person chooses to play is very telling. You could speculate about the difference between a person who played a trumpet compared with one who chose to play a harp.

Perhaps, in realising that you don't need to do a great deal of writing, you are now beginning to feel excited rather than intimidated at the thought of creating your Gift. If working on your Gift is pleasurable then you are much more likely to complete it. You could consider it like keeping fit. If you find a form of exercise that you really enjoy you are much more likely to stay with it than if you are having, each day, to force yourself to do something from which you derive no pleasure. To produce your Gift you don't even have to work at it day after day. A few hours spent one weekend using these guidelines would be enough.

What you produce will, of course, be very personal and unique, so you will need, right at the start, to make a few decisions.

How Much Time Would You Like to Commit to the Project?

Is it something you would like to complete in a few hours or do you want to make it a time-consuming hobby with a view to producing a wealth of information? It could be that you start off in a small way but enjoy the project so much that you move on to writing your memoirs in full.

The amount of effort you put into your Gift will depend on how interested you are in the project and how much time you have to devote to it. The point which cannot be emphasised too strongly is that even a very small amount of information, if it is presented in a way that is easy for your descendants to identify as important and to store, will become a valuable family heirloom. If you want to spend more time and go into more detail, so much the better.

Are you simply going to record something of your own life and what you know of your family in the immediate past or would you like to research your family tree back through the generations? Again, you might start by jotting down just what you know, decide you'd like to ask relatives, and then be unable to resist researching further.

What Form Would You Like Your Gift to Take?

This book aims to help you think about what form your Gift could take and how you would like it to develop. Of course, you could discover that you start with one plan and then change your mind as you go along - that's fine!

Future generations will learn a lot about your creativity and your personality because these will be reflected in the way in which you choose to present your Gift. For example:

  • If you are a photographer then photographs may play an important part.
  • If you have artistic flair then the way in which you present your Gift will reflect this, and the work could even be illustrated with your own drawings/paintings.

17

- If you are comfortable working on a computer, then your work can be stored in this way, showing that you are adept at handling modern technology.

- If you are methodical then you could complete the *Information Sheets* which are found at the back of this book.

- If you find writing easy then your life story will be written in your own particular style and you might decide to commit yourself to writing a full autobiography. You may then choose not to use the *Information Sheets*.

- If you see life events as being important, your *Factual Information Sheets* (templates are provided) will be full of interesting details.

- If, on the other hand, you spend time reflecting on your feelings and relationships, then your *Thoughts & Feelings Information Sheets* will be comprehensive.

- If you value sentimental possessions and have methodically kept greetings cards and letters then you might choose to concentrate on the 'Treasure Box' section.

- If you have a strong spiritual side, you may send messages about yourself and your view of life to future generations, perhaps including your favourite pieces of music or poetry - or even a poem or song you have written yourself.

- If you are interested in, and know about, what is going on in the world, perhaps through involvement in politics or a local campaigning group, you might have a lot to say about the events and changes which have occurred during your lifetime.

- If you value your place within the family, you may choose to become the family's historian by researching the past and perhaps producing an extensive family tree.

After reading through these guidelines you will decide for yourself which areas of your life and times you wish to cover and what form you would like your Gift to take. This book is designed to give you a basic grounding in how you can use new technology such as your computer or camcorder in the project, but if you have a particular interest in expanding your knowledge, additional reading is suggested.

Just get started by imagining how the finished work could look as it sits in pride of place in the home of one of your family members somewhere in the world (or on another planet - who knows?) in say, 200 years time[1].

To Sum Up

• Producing your Gift will be fun and needn't be too time-consuming.

• It's not essential to do a lot of writing.

• Guidelines are given for creative ways of communicating what you want to say to your descendants.

• Decide how much time you want to devote to the project and what you want to include - but be prepared to change your mind.

---

[1] If we take the average life span as being between 70 and 80 years (older for women than for men) this will mean that your Gift might have passed through the hands of three generations of your family by then.

WHY PRESERVE YOUR
LIFE STORY?

You are Special and Your Life is of Interest

The starting point of your work on your Gift is that you are a special and unique individual and that you form part of an ongoing family, however small. You are special to those around you now and, if you let them know something about you, you will be special to the generations to come.

Even if you do not have children of your own, you could play an important role by producing a Gift for the descendants of other members of your family with whom you are close.

How much do you know about what your great-grandparents and great-aunts and uncles were like? If you are lucky you will have a photograph of them. You might know where they are buried and be able to visit their graves. You might know that you are like them in physical appearance. In exceptional circumstances you might even live in the same house where they spent their lives and even be surrounded by some of the same furniture. But for most people, knowledge of past family members, even those who died only a decade or two ago, is very limited indeed.

Would you like to know something of what your ancestors were like? Such knowledge would not only be very interesting, but it could also help you to understand a little more about yourself. If your forebears' lives are of interest to you then you could speculate that in future years your life - how you felt, what things were important to you, what you did - will be of interest to your descendants.

You are a Chapter in Your Children's History

Because of today's mobile society, families are often divided by miles - sometimes by oceans - and preserving your story will help your children to gain a sense of their place in the scheme of things. Understanding where they come from will help them to have a sense of strength and security.

Geneticists have, in recent years, been amassing evidence which indicates that genetic make-up plays an important role in shaping temperament and some aspects of behaviour. In the latter part of the 20th century, geneticists embarked on the task of mapping every gene of the human body and less than a decade later they were able to produce a Genome which identified every single gene. Conditions such as allergies, depression and alcoholism, as well as personality traits such as shyness and curiosity are, according to some research, passed down genetically through families.

Further, psychologists have long been interested in the ways in which early childhood experiences, usually within the family, have a strong influence on how people behave in adult life. A simple example: a child who is constantly criticised may well grow up with little confidence, whereas a child who is praised is more likely to be self-assured. Through the socialisation process, people learn how to be mothers and fathers as well as how to be husbands and wives. However hard they try to be different, individuals are largely stuck with the models they absorbed from their early family group. Social environmental influences are passed down the generations to compound genetic pre-dispositions. From this you will see that you could learn a lot about yourself by knowing something of the people in the past whose genes you share and whose family relationships laid the foundation of how you were brought up.

To Help Future Generations

How many years has it taken for you to become acquainted with all the things that make your life really worthwhile? It is a task that can take a lifetime. Writings that you find inspirational, music that moves you and favourite holiday places are just a few of the things which are uplifting and help you to transcend the mundane stresses of everyday life. Why not share these with future generations? Who knows, they might find them uplifting too - and, with your help, it won't take them a lifetime to find them. After all, one of the things that separates man from other living creatures is his ability to share life experiences through words. Use that ability now to convey to your descendants all those things which you have found make life worth living.

Similarly, it might be helpful for your descendants to know something about how you faced and overcame difficulties. If it is true that genetic pre-disposition and social influences within a family play a large part in the making of an individual, then your descendants might well experience some of the problems which you have had to face in life. Perhaps you found a cure for your migraines, overcame your shyness or alcoholism, or learned how to live with dyslexia or diabetes. Including this in your Gift might be painful for you but by revealing yourself in this way it could well be that some future family member will make a real and meaningful connection with you. You can be sure that by telling how you faced difficulties and worked on your personal problems you could provide hope and courage to your descendants.

Your Life is 'Social History'

In the past, history concerned itself with kings and queens, battles and conquests. More recently historians have begun to turn their attention to the lives of 'ordinary' people. There has been a tremendous interest in 'social' history - that is, in everyday life as it was lived in the past. Historical novels are popular. 'Living' museums have sprung up to show the lives of ordinary working people. Television documentaries tell of the day-to-day challenges faced by such groups as the Pilgrim Fathers. Stately homes and historic buildings are no longer visited as remote 'museums' but have come alive with people acting out the everyday lives of members of the household - from the wealthy landowners down to the kitchen girls and passing peddlers. The day-to-day life that you are living now will be the social history of the future.

Life at the beginning of the 21st century is exciting and very rapidly changing. The very fact that you were alive at the birth of the new millennium will make you special to family members in the future. You witnessed - albeit not necessarily first-hand - the destruction of the Twin Towers. Depending on how old you are, you may have shared the excitement of man's first steps on the Moon. You can be sure that the world in which your children grow up is far, far different from that in which you were raised. By commenting on how you experienced such things as the coming of the supermarket, of the Internet or, if you are old enough, of the motor car, you will be bringing to life something which, for future generations, will be history. If they are able to know something of how these changes affected the life of a direct ancestor this will make their history come alive and have far more impact. Preserve it now while it is happening!

As a Gift to Yourself Too

Looking at and recording aspects of yourself and your life will, hopefully, prove to be a self-affirming exercise. You will be saying to the world today and in the future, 'This is who I am.' Social workers use 'Life Story' work to help children who are going through life changes to come to terms with the past and build towards the future. Similarly, you might like to see the project as a way of looking at your life so far, considering lessons learnt and planning any changes you could make. This could be the case at whatever age you decide to start work on your Gift but would be especially helpful if you are going through a significant life change. Perhaps your children have recently left home or you have started a new job in a different part of the country away from your family and friends, or perhaps you have just retired. Working on your Gift will give you the opportunity to make an assessment right now about who you are, where you are going and what your values are - a real Gift to yourself!

By recording something of your life and times you will be leaving a part of yourself behind after your death. Your life will be recalled in a small way each time your Gift is either looked at or read. You will have attained some degree of immortality. You might well feel a little embarrassed at acknowledging this as part of your reason for working on the project, but there is no need to - it is a strong and natural urge.

To Sum Up

Spend some time preserving something of your life and times because:

• You are special and your life will be of interest to members of your family in the future.

• It is likely that your descendants will be, in some respects, similar to yourself and may face some of the same opportunities and challenges.

• At the dawn of the second millennium the world is changing very rapidly. Your descendants will be intrigued to find out what the world was like in your time and what changes were significant for you.

• The project is a way of valuing what you have in your life and planning for the future.

AT WHAT AGE SHOULD YOU START WORK ON YOUR GIFT?

If you are wondering whether the time is right to start working on your Gift then the answer is, 'Yes - there's no time like the present.'

If you choose to make the production of your Gift an ongoing project, you can add bits as you go through life and as you have the time and inclination. It is likely that many people won't start until they are into middle age or perhaps when they retire. Retirement is the life stage when most people start to have more time to spare and perhaps begin to think about what has been happening in their lives, but this is by no means the only time to embark on such a project.

What then are the advantages of beginning the work at different times in your life?

At Birth

Your Gift would be very comprehensive if someone else (possibly a grandparent) started it for you when you were born (more about this later). In that way they could include something about your birth, early years and schooling, and then you could take it over when you were old enough.

When You Are Young

There are obvious advantages to starting when you are young:

- You may well be in contact with grandparents and even great-grandparents - a valuable source of information.
- Your parents are more likely to be around which gives you access to information about your birth and early childhood.
- Primary source material, such as old school reports, is likely to be available.
- Memories of early childhood will be fresher in your mind and you might be in a position to take a photograph of your first home or school.
- You will be able to update your Gift as events happen and so information will be more immediate and accurate.
- If you keep a diary or journal you can ensure that it is recorded on archive-quality paper and stored in conditions that will maximise the chance of it lasting well into the future.

In Later Life

There are also advantages to starting later in life, whether in middle age or when you are older:

- You are likely to have a more balanced, mature picture of your life overall, especially when it comes to identifying changes that have been significant.
- You are more likely to complete the task. Although your past life will have to be recorded retrospectively, and the memories may have faded a little, it is all there and is available for consideration and for recording in some way. This means that you could complete the Gift in a weekend, possibly adding to it as the years go by. The younger person will have to wait for their life to unfold before they can tell their full story.

• If you are retired you may have more time to devote to your Gift.

• If you are past your youth you will have a good picture of how the world has changed during your lifetime.

So, whatever your age, get started right now!

To Sum Up

• Ideally, start recording life events for new members of the family when (or before) they are born.

• If you start your Gift when you are a young adult you will:

  - have valuable primary source materials available
  - be able to record events more accurately as they happen
  - be able to save photographs and other ephemera before they deteriorate and can keep them in the best conditions.

• If you start later in life you:

  - may have more time to spare
  - are likely to have a more balanced picture of your life and the changes in the world which have been significant for you.

• Whatever your age, start now!

A WORD ABOUT
THE EMOTIONAL IMPACT

Before you start working on your Gift, take time to think about what impact the project could have both on yourself and on other members of your family. First, how do you think you might feel as you look back over your life? There is no doubt that, whatever your age, examining your life and deciding what you would like to record for future generations could stir strong emotions in you.

If you decide to research your family history you might begin to feel in some way in touch with past family members. This could give you a sense of security, knowing that your life fits into an ongoing family saga stretching back in time and forward into the future. It could also bring a feeling of sadness about times past and about people who are no longer with you. You might feel anger at the way you were treated as a child, or regret that you did not treat your parents as you perhaps now feel you should have done. As you review your past you might feel pride at the things you have achieved in your life. On the other hand, you might regret missed opportunities.

Whether you are sorting through piles of photographs and video cassettes, talking to elderly relatives, or thinking about your own parents, you should be prepared for the emotions that are likely to be stirred. You will probably be surprised by how much you have done! If you are in your middle years it is sometimes easy to wonder what you have done with your life - many people feel they have underachieved and not done enough. A look back through old photo albums is usually all that it takes to give you a sense of having been around. If you have had just one holiday a year it is surprising how many places you can visit in a lifetime! If you take pictures when you are out with the family or at Christmas, you have a lot of fun events recorded.

Then there is the sadness of change. If you are in your 30s you may feel sad about the old school friends with whom you've lost touch - friends who were once very important to you. If you are in your 40s or 50s and your children are leaving home, you may be reminded of that playhouse which took you so long to make but is long since gone.

Because you won't want your Gift to be nostalgically stuck in the past, it is important that it also represents what is going on in the *present*. Endow it with a sense of moving forward. For example, if you love camping and have included photographs of camping holidays at home and abroad, your caption could read: 'I have always enjoyed camping and am continually looking for new places to explore.' Or perhaps your first grandchild has just been born. The caption, written in the present, could read: 'This is our much wanted grandson Samuel, taken soon after he was born. We enjoy looking after him each Wednesday afternoon.' This gives a reader in the future a sense of time and movement.

Whatever form your Gift takes, whether it is a photo album, a Treasure Box, a Life Book or whatever, it should be accompanied by a note stating when it was initially started so that the recipient will have a sense of how the project progressed. Such a note could read:

I decided to start this Life Book in the year 2002 when I reached the age of 50 and my first grandchild was born. For me he represents the future. I began to think that I would like to record and preserve what I know of our family history and my own life as part of that ongoing story. I intend to continue to update my story as the years go by and would like to leave it to my children (and their children) in the hope that they will take pleasure in it and enjoy love, peace and the richness of life.

With much love,
(Full Name and Date)

Questions of Honesty and Hurt

Next, you will need to think about how your Gift will be received by members of your family. How you choose to record the character of your family and the world in which you are living is *your* perspective, *your* version of events. By its very nature it will be subjective; it will reflect how you see things. Your version might not be quite the same as that of other family members. It could be that while you are working on your project you begin to feel that what you are conveying might cause certain people to feel sadness or anger. Where you feel there is a risk of hurting family members by revealing contentious information or past disputes, be guided by a sense of kindness and adopt an approach of avoiding hurt to others.

You might decide that you would like to discuss what you are writing with other people who have been involved, or that might be too difficult. Skeletons in the cupboard should be dealt with sensitively - or not at all! - when you are consulting with relations on family history, particularly if they are elderly and have grown up in an era very different from your own. Remember that time has changed social perceptions of such things as illegitimate births or co-habiting 'out of wedlock'. Many arrangements previously seen as social taboos or serious transgressions are now part of day-to-day life in many modern cultures and go without question.

Because you are preserving the present for the benefit of future generations, you owe it to them to be as honest as you can. Try to be truthful about your upbringing. People sometimes see the past as they want to see it. Painful memories are repressed and a more acceptable picture is built up. If you were ashamed of your father's lowly occupation you might, in later life, say he was a 'farmer' when he was really a farm labourer. Ask yourself how the recipients of your Gift would be likely to remember you if they were to hear a different version of your past from another source. Remember, if you are found to have been less than truthful in one respect it will throw other things into question, and by the time your Gift is read you might not be around to explain yourself. Would you like your descendants to think of you as dishonest and snobbish or as truthful and down to earth?

If you feel that in order to pass down an accurate picture of yourself and your life you need to include some contentious material or to record some private part of yourself which you would not like to be seen by others in the present, you could include a 'Confidential' section to be kept private by someone you trust until all those who are involved have passed away. Or you could simply leave your Gift with your Will.

To Sum Up

- Your Gift might stir strong emotions in yourself and other family members.
- You could gain a sense of security by looking at your place within your family.
- Examining your life and that of your ancestors might make you feel fortunate, proud, sad or resentful.
- Try not to allow your Gift to get stuck in one time - give it a sense of moving forward as your life moves on.
- Recognise that your version of events might not be the same as that of other family members.
- Try to deal with family stories sensitively, taking into account the feelings of others.
- Be as honest as you can.
- If necessary, keep a 'Confidential' section which is not shown to anyone until all those concerned have passed away.

PART II

A PICTURE IS WORTH A THOUSAND WORDS

A PHOTOGRAPHIC RECORD OF YOUR LIFE

It has been said that 'a picture is worth a thousand words', so a very effective way to communicate the story of your life and times would be pictorially. Most people have photographs of some kind. Although it can be time-consuming, you might consider that a Life Photo Album would make an interesting Gift and would be worth all the time and effort.

If you take lots of photographs, there is every chance that while some are mounted in albums, many of them have been pushed into drawers and cupboards rarely to see the light of day. You may also have photographs of your parents, grandparents and, if you are lucky, your great-grandparents. Again, these may have been mounted in albums and labelled, but it is much more likely that they lie anonymously in some dark corner waiting to pass into oblivion. House clearance items in auction rooms often include old photographs, some of which date back to the latter years of the 19th century. What a pity that they have been lost by their families. Unless you act now, your family photographs will suffer a similar fate and will pass into the future unrecognised and unknown. By including them in your life collection you can ensure that they take their rightful place in your family history.

It is more than likely that any photographs you have already mounted in albums are rather quickly deteriorating because you have used modern albums with either plastic pockets or sheets of transparent film to hold the photographs in place on the page. Most standard-quality albums contain high percentages of lignin, acid and sulphur which will lead, even after short-term contact, to image fading and tone loss and will leave the photographs discoloured and brittle. It might be that you rarely look at your photo collection but when you do you will discover that many album pages and photographs have already become discoloured - even before they are much more than 10 years old. In addition, the transparent sheets are likely to have stuck to the photographs and much of the plastic will have become brittle.

Photographs that have been stored randomly in a drawer or cardboard box will have been exposed to dust which scratches the surface. Similarly, rifling through piles of old photographs leads to scratched surfaces, torn corners, and creases and folds. What a disappointment - there's not much hope that these photographs, inappropriately mounted in albums or randomly stored in drawers, will be around in 200 years time!

If you decide to produce a photographic record of your life and times, your first decision will be which photographs to include. The number of photos you use will, of course, be determined by the size of the album you choose. You could decide to produce a relatively small album, say about 20 pages of A5 size, or you could be more ambitious and go for something larger, perhaps 40 pages of A4. You could choose to make up a very concise collection with maybe just one photograph representing each period of your life, or you might compile a larger album which says more about you.

Try, however, to keep the collection relatively small - it is more likely to survive if it is easy for your descendants to store.

Given that most people have hundreds of photographs to choose from, how do you go about selecting those that say the most about you and your life and times? Remember that your aim is to convey the essence of your life to your descendants. Try to put them in your shoes. Convey the emotion of the event. A good starting-point would be to consider this question – 'If I were to be presented with a photo album of my grandparents' lives, what would I like to be included in it?' You would probably like to know about their parents and grandparents, and that would almost certainly be of interest to your own descendants too. So, you can start the story of your life and times, before you were born, by including a selection of photographs of your own ancestors. By doing this you will be ensuring that they play a part in the story of your family history and will prevent them from being lost to anonymity forever.

You might find selecting photographs of your ancestors difficult, especially if the pictures that are in the best condition are the least interesting. In the second half of the 19th century and, more commonly, in the early years of the 20th century, many people donned their Sunday best and went off to have a professional photograph taken. There must be thousands of photographs in existence that look very similar - the women in their long skirts and tight bodices and the men in high-necked collars and suits with a waistcoat, often embellished with a watch and chain. The family group or an individual would be carefully posed against a backcloth, perhaps with a picture either of the country or seaside, and would be staring intently at the camera.

These pictures are usually good for spotting family likenesses - the tall stature, the distinguished nose, the lopsided mouth - but otherwise say very little about the individual. It is true that the very fact they had a photograph taken says something about their class status. Members of the lower working classes at that time would not have had the money or time available to take themselves off to a photographer's studio. It is surprising, however, how many people from fairly 'ordinary' backgrounds have photographs, taken around 1900, of their family members looking very smart. Perhaps being able to afford to go to a photographer's studio was something that working people aspired to as a sign of some status.

You can perhaps date the photograph by the name of the studio, which was often printed on the back. A local museum might be able to throw more light on the period the photograph was taken, getting clues from the props and paraphernalia in the pictures or from the clothes.

Soon after 1900, Kodak introduced their simple and inexpensive cameras and people started to take 'snaps' when they were out and about enjoying themselves. Although formal photographs have their place in family history, 'snaps' taken during a day at the seaside or enjoying a game of cricket are likely to tell you more about the lives of your forebears.

After you have selected the photographs of your ancestors that you want to include in your Gift, you can then move on to choose photographs that represent you at different times in your life. Try to include pictures that clearly show how you look. This is especially important because your descendants will be interested to see how your physical features resemble theirs. You could take some photographs of yourself specially for the purpose of showing your true physical characteristics, with a front view and a side view. In this way future family historians will be able to identify family traits and see in what way, if any, they take after you.

Other photographs could show:

- A house where you spent much of your life - outside and inside views. A shot of the back of the house and photographs of particular areas like the kitchen and sitting room might be especially telling.

• Places you have lived. If there have been dramatic changes in the areas you have inhabited during your lifetime, you could show these with your photographs. For example, you might be lucky enough to have a photograph of yourself as a child playing in the road outside your house with not a car in sight. If this is a road that has, in more recent years, become a busy thoroughfare throbbing with traffic, the contrast will be of interest to future generations. Or you might once have lived in a quiet rural area with trees and country lanes, which has more recently been developed. Similarly interesting would be small corner shops where now a huge supermarket stands, or a village pond that has now given way to a housing estate.

• The school you attended - once again, outside and inside views. A picture of your school uniform and perhaps an area like the sports hall or science laboratory would say a lot about life at school. You could also get permission to take some pictures of your own children or grandchildren at school, hopefully covering everything from play group or nursery to university. The contrast between your school environment and theirs would most likely fascinate your descendants.

• Particular clothes that you like. Include both leisure and formal wear - perhaps a picture of you in your badminton kit and/or dressed up for a big occasion, say a family wedding.

• Jobs that you have had. This is especially interesting if the technology used for a particular kind of work has changed a lot during your working life. For example, if you were a typist, and started work in the 1950s, your work would have been made progressively easier, first by the electrification of typewriters and then by the advent of word processors. Most types of work have been affected by change during the second half of the 20th century, and many jobs have disappeared completely. Jobs in manufacturing industries and in agriculture have declined in number and there has been a huge growth in service industries. If you are lucky, you will have photographs showing yourself employed in a now much changed or non-existent job and your descendants would be interested to see any pictures you can include which show these changes.

• Holiday and leisure snaps. Now that many people spend their holidays jetting around the world, it will be interesting for your descendants to see how you were able to enjoy yourself at a seaside resort not far from your home town or having a picnic in the countryside. Swimming fashions, too, will be especially interesting, as will the fact that until around the 1950s, people often went for a day at the seaside wearing their Sunday best. For the vast majority of people, informal clothes - apart from working clothes - were unknown before around the middle of the 20th century!

To Sum Up

• Producing a Life Photo Album could be time-consuming but the result would be worth the effort.
• Many interesting, old, unlabelled photographs are lying haphazardly, deteriorating rapidly, in the back of a cupboard

- archive them now to prevent them being lost to your family.

• Your Life Photo Album is more likely to be valued and kept by your descendants if it is reasonably concise and easy to store.

• Begin telling your story before you were born by including photographs of your own forebears.

• Try to select only photographs that say something about you and your times.

CREATING AND PRESERVING YOUR LIFE PHOTO ALBUM

Having chosen your photographs for inclusion in your Life Photo Album you will now move on to consider how to present them in such a way that they look attractive, while at the same time maximising their chance of surviving into the future.

Displaying your Photographs

Unfortunately, photo albums that are generally available in the shops, although they are pretty and serve their purpose, do not generally make any pretence at being archival quality. These albums are unlikely to be made from acid-free paper or cardboard, and the plastic sheets will probably contain chemicals that will damage the photographs in quite a short time. So you will have to be prepared to spend the extra money needed to buy an archival-quality album or some other materials for displaying your photographs.

One option is to purchase an archival photo album from a reputable specialist (see addresses in Appendix 2). You will then also need to use archival-quality adhesive corners. If you use any glue, be sure that it is acid-free, non-caustic and with a neutral pH level of 7.0. Alternatively, photographs can be mounted on acid-free paper or board, which you should then slip into a polyester sleeve. Again, since some grades of polyester contain plasticisers that will damage photographs, every effort should be made to acquire archival-quality polyester sleeves. Sheets can then be housed in a folder and kept in a side-opening box made from high-quality materials.

Having purchased the necessary storage materials, it is now time to place your selected photographs in some sort of order. The most obvious way would be to set them in chronological order, perhaps with headings such as: Ancestry; Early years; Growing up; Career; Marriage and young married life; Family life etc... If you have had a long-standing hobby or something that has been very important to you, you might also choose to have a section devoted solely to that aspect of your life.

Captions can be placed alongside the photographs, again using acid-free paper or labels held in place by adhesive corners. Alternatively, you could write directly onto the page, making sure that you use long-lasting ink. It is better not to write on the back of photographs, but if you feel you would like to then do use a soft pencil and a very light touch.

A good way of identifying people in a large group photograph is to follow this procedure:

- Take a photocopy of the original photograph.
- Using the copy, trace the outline of each person onto a piece of acid-free paper, to be used as a caption for the photograph.
- Number each person within their outline.
- Add a 'key' which ascribes a name to each number.

While you are collating your photographs, avoid using paper-clips or pins or any sort of glues or adhesives. It is also important to avoid handling the prints too much - the photographs will be damaged by any dirt, perspiration salts and greasy deposits that are transferred from your hands. You can buy thin cotton gloves which will prevent your fingerprints from leaving damaging marks.

A Computerised Version

There are advantages to organising your photographs on a computer. A very large collection of photographs (and your other computer files, e.g. text) can be stored on just one CD-Rom, and a back-up copy and further copies can be made, without loss of quality, for family members to share.

Photos from a digital camera are, of course, by their very nature, suitable for storing on computer files. Conventional photos can be scanned and saved in a suitable format - JPEG is commonly used as it keeps the file size as small as possible. It is best to organise little collections of photograph files into folders, with appropriate names for both the folders and each photograph. Any photo-editing software will provide a means of adding captions, but the filename itself can serve this purpose.

Ideally, your CD-Rom should be kept with the original photograph album. Do not assume that computer-stored information is necessarily longer lasting than the original material. You should remember that a great deal of uncertainty surrounds the question of how long this media will last, so don't rely on it. You should also attach a note to your package asking your descendants to transfer the material onto any new system as information technology develops.

Preservation

You can't aim for perfection in preserving your photographs, but you can certainly take a few important steps to give them a good chance of lasting well into the future. Without a great deal of effort, money and space, it is unlikely that you will be able to create museum-quality archival conditions, but if you follow a few basic rules and are prepared to spend a little money, your photographs will be more able to stand the test of time.

Condition of Pictures

In recent years there has been considerable interest in family history and people have been digging out their old photographs, many of which are already in a state of some deterioration - perhaps through fading or physical damage of some kind. Professional photographers have become adept at meeting the need for renovation work. It's amazing what a professional photograph restorer can do to enhance apparently hopelessly faded images and even re-build areas of photographs that have been damaged. Images are sharpened, contrast is enhanced and half-missing faces are re-built. If you have a computer and scanner and the necessary software this is something you might attempt yourself, particularly if all that is required is the elimination of small cracks and scratches. Photoshop is one of the better-known applications for this work. If your computer skills are not so advanced, however, employing the skills of a professional restorer is a very worthwhile venture.

Storage Conditions

This is where you can really enhance your photographs' chances of survival. Where you store your photograph collection will have a huge affect on its chances of survival. Photographs deteriorate if they are exposed to moisture, fluctuations of temperature, sunlight, atmospheric pollutants, handling and inappropriate mounting materials such as adhesives and albums. Experts recommend a temperature below 18°C and a humidity level of between 30%-50% for black and white photographs. Most people's homes will provide just these conditions. Colour photographs should be stored in cooler conditions - between 2°C and 10°C with a humidity level of 20%-40%. The most important point is that storage conditions should be stable - without too much fluctuation in temperature or humidity. Photographs should not be stored in damp cellars or warm attics; neither should they be displayed over open fires and radiators or in unventilated bathrooms. The garage is another storage area to be avoided.

If you like the idea of keeping a photographic record of your life, your aim could be that by the time you reach your later years you will have an illustrated compact volume to leave behind. Then your family, while clearing your possessions after your death, won't have to decide which of your tens of photo albums and piles of old photographs to preserve - they will simply keep and treasure the one marked, 'The Life and Times of __'.

To Sum Up

• In making a photographic record of your life and times you will need to select, mount and label a concise collection of photographs.

• You should only use archival-quality materials for your collection.

• For each photograph be sure to make a label which clearly identifies the subjects.

• If possible, make a computerised copy of your work - and remember to attach a note asking your descendants to update it as new technology supersedes the old.

• Pay due attention to the conditions in which the collection will be stored.

YOUR CHILDREN'S STORY

You will by now be aware of the fact that it is very difficult to remember what was happening to you and in the world around you when you were a small child. Information about your early years, where you were born, your first day at school and so on, may well be buried in your unconscious, but most of it is not available to the conscious memory. To fill in the picture, you will have to rely on older people who were around when you were a child - parents, older siblings or perhaps grandparents. Similarly, your descendants will have to rely on you to fill in this missing picture concerning their early years.

Most people have piles of photographs of their children and grandchildren but these are often stored rather haphazardly. Baby record books are a favourite gift for a new baby, and parents and grandparents proudly record baby's birth weight, first steps and first birthday party. Every move of a first child or grandchild is usually avidly recorded, often in albums which are pretty but not necessarily archivally sound. Enthusiasm can wane as the child gets older, and the lives of subsequent children and grandchildren are often not recorded in any structured way.

The problem is - how much of this information is going to survive? The answer is probably 'very little'. How useful and interesting it would be then, if you laid the foundation for your own child's (or grandchild's) 'Gift for the Future' now. A good way to do this would be to start a Life Photo Album for the child by finding a very sturdy archivally-sound photo album and putting into it some photographs going back to before the baby was born. You would then update it as time goes by.

You could include photographs (accompanied by a few well-chosen words) of:

- Any ancestor about whom you have any knowledge - parents, grandparents and, hopefully, great-grandparents. You could also write a few words about any known ancestor of whom you do not have a photograph
- The parent's wedding
- The child's place of birth
- The baby soon after birth
- The young family
- The child's first school
- A family holiday
- Later schools
- Early adulthood - around 18

It is important to bear in mind that you need only record very basic information to build the foundation of a pictorial history of the child's life. The first 18 years could take up, say, about 15 pages of an album. What a lovely present to hand over on an 18th birthday! If you have chosen a fairly large archive-quality album, your child/grandchild will be able to continue to keep his or her Life Photo Album in the years to follow.

When a couple are getting married, a joint Life Book would make a very symbolic gift. Before the wedding, you could contact the prospective in-laws and ask if they could let you have a selection of photographs of the bride or groom from birth, through childhood, up to the present. It's nicer to keep the album as a surprise if possible, so don't ask the bridal couple themselves.

You will then have to set about the task of compiling the album and most of the ideas already discussed will apply. Put photographs of the bride at the front of the album and those of the groom at the back; the two will then meet in the middle where space can be left for a small collection of wedding photographs. A nice idea would be to pass the album round to guests at the wedding reception.

Remember, it is well worth spending money on a proper archive-quality album and, as the album is to be a gift, you might like to make or buy an attractive bag or box in which to keep it.

To Sum Up

• Babies and young children may be unable to recall their early years later in life.

• You can help them to build their own 'Gift for the Future' by making a pictorial record of events in their lives as they happen.

- Choose just one photograph of each of their ancestors and of each 'episode' of their lives.
- Include a few words about known ancestors of whom you do not have a photograph.
- Use an archival-quality album.
- If you are very selective you should be able to cover the first 18 years in about 15 pages.
- Present the album to the child on his or her 18th birthday.

A VIDEO RECORDING

It is usually the case that while professionally made films can be so engrossing, amateur videos are often much less so. If you choose to make one or more video recordings as part of your Gift you will need to make sure that they hold the interest of your future audience. Of course, you might already be a very proficient video maker in which case you are all set to produce a video package of your life and times. If, however, you don't feel too confident behind the camcorder, it would be worth taking a few steps towards improving your technique.

Looking for Material from the Past

You should start by looking at any existing material that may be suitable for inclusion in your Gift - video cassettes accumulated by yourself and by other family members who might have footage of your ancestors and of your early years. You might also come across some old cine film. If you wish you can combine video and cine film footage and even still photographs.

Much of what has been said earlier about photographs applies to your videos. If you have a large collection of video cassettes it is possible that you have meticulously edited them, labelled them and stored them in an orderly fashion, but it is much more likely that they are piled high in a cupboard somewhere waiting for the day when you will get around to sorting them out. In reality this probably means that they are waiting for the day in years to come when a relative of yours has the unenviable task of sorting out your things after your death and they are taken to the local rubbish tip. Valuable family history will be lost forever!

Each video, moreover, is probably unedited. A recording of a holiday in Disney World lasts for two or three hours and an amateur wedding video probably shows every part of the day in minute detail. An additional frustration for future viewers is that the people on the videos are probably not identified clearly - if at all.

Editing and Collating Material from the Past

Having assembled all the available materials, how do you go about producing a concise, interesting compilation which represents your life up to the present? It's best to transform all of your recordings into just one video format. Digital video format is best as it lends itself to easy editing. A lot of home-use computers are now capable of reading VHS recordings and converting them to digital format.

Cine film can be 'captured' simply by projecting it onto a screen and recording it with a tripod mounted camcorder. If you want to include still photographs in your video presentation, these can also be recorded with a camcorder. Once captured in this way, if you have suitable editing software, you are ready to prepare your video Gift.

The completed package could then be transferred onto DVD, although there is likely to be some expense with this. The advantage is that it will then be very stable and however many times it is played or copied it should not deteriorate in quality. It seems likely that before long DVD recorders will become affordable to the amateur enthusiast.

Enlisting the Help of a Professional

You may, of course, prefer to discuss your project with a professional video producer. Someone with the right equipment and knowledge could take the old cine film, still photographs and video recordings that you have chosen and turn them into a neat package illustrating the story of you and your family's life so far. You will be very impressed with what can be achieved by an experienced operator, editing with a computer and adding background music and/or a voice-over to explain what is going on. For a relatively modest cost you could have all the old family material transformed into a neat package which would make a very compact Gift for the Future and a very welcome gift for a family member in the present!

What Should You Include?

So much video footage is just the result of someone picking up the camera and recording what is going on, without a great deal of art or thought. Much of the available material, whether it be on video or cine film, will be of only limited interest to your descendants. Hence the need for good editing of any material. Remember that the aim is to keep the completed package compact.

If you are lucky enough to have any cine film or video footage of your parents or grandparents, you could start your video package with 'Ancestry' and then move through 'Birth and early life' to 'School years', 'Working life', 'Marriage and children', 'Retirement' and so on. Compile a collection that covers your life so far, ensuring that each 'episode' - say a new baby, a first day at school, or a wedding - lasts no more than about 10 minutes. An alternative approach would be to have separate cassettes for 'Holidays', 'Special occasions', 'Hobbies' or anything else that you feel says something about your life and the times in which you are living.

In deciding what to include, remember that as well as being interested in the people who are the subject matter of your video, your descendants will be looking for evidence of how the world looked in times gone by. So, if you have footage of your family on a trip to the beach, include each family member but also, if possible, show the car you travelled in, the restaurant where you had lunch, the ice-cream vendor and the general appearance of the houses and shops close to the beach. Social historians looking at private collections of old cine film and video footage often feel very frustrated because the camera focuses only on the people, without taking in the surroundings.

Bear in mind the following points when you are selecting material:

An Early Baby Video

Future viewers will no doubt be interested in how you were dressed as a baby and in the furniture, toys and general surroundings. They will also be on the lookout for family likenesses. But unlimited footage of the baby's babbling and early attempts to sit up, crawl and walk will eventually become tedious.

So remember the golden rule - keep the episodes concise!

Wedding Videos

These will probably be of great interest. Changing fashions in wedding clothes are fascinating to observe, and most people - especially women! - enjoy a good wedding. As part of your Gift it will be specially interesting because lots of members of the family are gathered together at the same time. However, many of the things that go on at weddings - the feasting, speeches, dancing and drinking - have stayed much the same over time and will probably change very little in the future. The fashions and surroundings will be interesting and you should make sure that you include shots of the things that are most likely to change, for instance the car the bride came to the church in. Just remember that interest will wane if every detail from dawn till dusk is included.

Holiday Videos

Much of what has been said about baby and wedding videos applies here. Initial interest will be concentrated on identifying which of the 'players' in the video are ancestors of the viewer, on the fashions of the day and on the surroundings. If the holiday destination is familiar to the viewer they will also be interested to see how much it has changed.

An Interview

In addition to these obvious choices, you might choose to record an interview with someone - perhaps a grandparent. If you ask your grandparent about his or her parents and early life you will be recording visually something valuable about your ancestry.

(For ideas on what to include in your interview see the section, 'An Audio Record' in Part IV.)

Having combined and edited the videos that tell your life story into a compact package you are now ready to think about how to record events in the future with a view to continuing the story.

To Sum Up

• Go through any of your old videos (and cine film) and edit them to make a compact story of your life up until now.

• Throw your net wider by looking at any videos that your parents or other relatives might have.

• You could also include some still photographs in your video.

• You might have the necessary equipment and experience to make a video compilation yourself - if not, take your material to a professional video maker to do the editing and collating work.

• The best way to ensure that your material is stable and durable is to transfer it to DVD.

MAKING AND KEEPING VIDEO RECORDINGS

Now that you have a compilation of your life to date you are ready to think about producing an ongoing record of the future as it unfolds.

How much time will the average amateur video maker put into creating video recordings? They will usually invest some time in studying how to operate the controls of their new camcorder, but for many this will be the extent of their learning about video making. It's easy to assume that making a video is just a question of common sense and that all you have to do is alternate still close-ups and distance shots with a bit of panning and zooming. If you can admit that you are guilty of this approach then be assured that you can make far better videos by investing a small amount of time and effort in learning about video making.

You might decide to join a club or class dedicated to video making or do some more reading on the subject (see Appendix 1), but unless you want to make video making a serious hobby that isn't necessary. Whatever the subject matter, if you have studied your handbook and have a good understanding of how your camcorder works, you can easily learn a few fairly straightforward techniques that will help you to produce a video recording of which you can be proud.

Planning

For each video sequence, try to plan what you want to record and how you intend to go about it. Think about dividing the occasion up into episodes, recording one episode and then stopping before moving on to the next. A common fault with the amateur video maker is that the whole video is one long shot zooming in and out, panning from left to right, moving from one situation to another with no cut-off points between sequences - rather like a book that is one long chapter.

Timing

Focusing too long on a single shot is another very common fault in amateur video making. If you are videoing the school Christmas concert or sports day you will be tempted to hold the camera on your child in case something interesting happens, but most shots, if there is little action, will become boring after around 15-20 seconds.

Long, Mid or Short Shots

Long and mid shots and close-ups are used to different effect and an appreciation of how changing the length of focus helps the cohesion of the video will give a better result.

Long shots, which present the total scene, are a good way of introducing the viewer to a situation. If you were recording in a children's playground, your introductory long-distance shots would take in the whole play area and all the children playing there. Long shots can also close an episode by gently zooming out away from the subject. Hollywood Westerns often used this technique to end a film, with the hero riding out into the prairie. Long shots should be used sparingly, however, because they distance the viewer from the subject.

Most commonly used is the mid shot, which means that the subjects - usually people - can be seen clearly while still leaving enough space to take in the situation in which the action is being played out. To go back to the playground project, your mid shots would home in on your child climbing up a piece of playground equipment or sitting on a swing.

You can then use close-up shots to concentrate attention on one subject, or even a part of one subject. Close-ups can have great visual and emotional impact and bring the viewer physically and emotionally closer to the action. Professional film makers often zoom in on someone's eyes to indicate tension in the situation. A close-up shot of the face of a child on a swing would reveal the laughter and joy, which would help to convey the excitement of the moment in a way that would not be so obvious from a more distant shot.

Zooming

The zoom lens is indispensable in adding interest by way of changing from distance shots to close-ups, although you can also physically move yourself so that you are either closer to, or further away from, your subject. Don't over-use the zoom lens though; it can become annoying for viewers if you are constantly zooming in and out.

Composition

Whether you are painting a picture, taking a photograph or making a video recording, the success of the finished result will largely depend on how much attention you pay to composition. It is relatively easy to compose a still photograph but, because a video lasts longer, problems can arise which disturb the composition of the frame you are filming. To start with, the subject is likely to move, so it is important to position him or her away from the edge of the frame - otherwise, a slight movement might mean you lose half a body. Before you start, take a look around to make sure there is nothing that is likely to encroach on the scene - perhaps some children playing nearby, or a dog. When you frame the subject make sure that no unwanted bits of people or buildings intrude round the edges. Use the zoom to eliminate any unwanted distractions.

Reframing

A trick worth remembering is that each time you choose a scene that you would like to film, you can compose the shot with the camcorder in pause mode. Then, when you switch on to record, the camcorder will have set the correct exposure and focus point.

Movement

Another common fault in amateur video making is camera shake. This can be off-putting for the viewer. It's quite difficult to hold a camcorder still for long periods of time, although the latest equipment is much lighter and thus easier to manage. The latest digital camcorders are very small and they are constantly shrinking in size as technology advances. Using a tripod, if it has a tilt and pan facility, you will, with practise, be able to eliminate camera shake. If you don't have a tripod an alternative is the kind of single, telescopic leg support which stills cameramen sometimes use. If no such equipment is available then look around for a wall or horizontal surface to support your arms.

Sound

The visual aspect of a video tells only half the story, so if you want to turn out a first-class recording you must pay attention to the sound track. Begin by listening carefully for any background noises that might distract attention and do what you can to eliminate them. You might have to put off doing the recording if, for example, a neighbour is making a lot of noise mowing his lawn. Or you might have to begin again if a car suddenly starts up nearby. If you are recording what someone is saying, it is best to let them finish before cutting, but if you are not able to do this you might later be able to edit the video when there appears to be a natural break in the conversation.

If you are recording outdoors you should take some steps to ensure that the sound quality is as you want it. If there is a lot of wind you could ask someone to protect you by holding a golfing umbrella. You could also ask anyone who is talking to speak more loudly and clearly to ensure that they are heard above background noise. If you have a camcorder with headphone sockets you will be able to hear precisely what is being recorded.

You might think that shooting indoors would be easier but this is not always the case. The recording level automatically increases when there is little noise and decreases when there is a lot of sound, so if you are shooting where there is very little sound you have to be careful not to bump the camcorder or shuffle your feet as this will be picked up by the microphone. Similarly, household sounds which are so familiar to you that you do not notice them - such as a clock ticking or the central heating clicking on and off - can sound very loud when picked up by the camcorder microphone. For shooting indoors you will also have to be aware of the acoustic environment in which you are recording. Hard surfaces such as windows, wooden and plastic furniture, plaster walls and wooden doors reflect the sound and produce a lot of echo, whereas carpets and soft furnishings absorb the sound and produce a more muted effect.

In addition to thinking about eliminating unwanted noise interference, it is worth spending some time deciding what sound track you would like to include. If you are interviewing someone you should practise with the sound to make sure that both the interviewer and the interviewee can be heard equally plainly. With an event such as a wedding you might choose to say something about the people and what is going on - in a voice just loud enough to be recorded by the camcorder's microphone.

Editing

You stand the best chance of producing a worthwhile video recording if you familiarise yourself with your system's editing facility and edit your material rigorously so that you clean up unwanted intrusions and lengthy sequences that threaten to become boring.

It is also important that viewers are able to identify who is on the video and what is happening. A title card naming either the year or the event should announce each new episode. The title can be created either electronically, using a title superimposer, or you can simply stick white letters onto a dark background and shoot them. Another approach would be to use something that is associated with the event you are videoing, perhaps a birth announcement card or a wedding invitation. The wording on the card would then make a good caption in itself. Perhaps the best way to ensure that the viewer knows what is going on and can keep track of events as they happen is to have an ongoing commentary.

A last word about technique: don't practise your new skills at a very important family occasion - leave those to the professionals until you are more confident and experienced - to avoid disappointment.

How to Store Your Videos

It is very important that after paying so much attention to producing your video cassettes you think about how to maximise their durability.

There are two aspects of video cassettes to consider - the magnetic coating which enables the data to be stored on the tape, and the polyester base which makes up the tape itself. Video cassettes would be ruined if you were to pass a magnet over them, and you should ensure that they are stored away from any strong source of magnetism such as a television. It is known that the polyester base has a long life, but the data is most likely to be lost by the magnetic layer coming away from the base.

Another thing to consider is that the technology itself is rapidly changing. It's no good putting video cassettes away in a cupboard somewhere, assuming that they will be ready for viewing 50 years from now. You could consult a professional to see if you could have any material currently stored on video transferred to DVD, although, as has already been mentioned, the longevity of much computer-stored data is still open to question. The most important thing is to ensure that your cassettes are carefully labelled, asking your descendants to transfer them on to more up-to-date media as it becomes available. The label should be big and bold and marked 'IMPORTANT' to ensure it catches attention.

Finally, the quality of video recorded material will deteriorate each time you play it, so save viewings for special occasions!

To Sum Up

• Before you start, take some steps to improve your video-making technique.

• Supplement the visual information with an audio commentary identifying people and places.

• Be sure to label each episode in your recording carefully.

• Don't expose video cassettes to any strong source of magnetism such as a television.

• Carefully label your cassettes, asking your descendants to upgrade as new technology becomes available.

• Don't keep watching your videos - they will deteriorate each time they are played.

A WORD ABOUT IMAGES

Technological development has meant that over the years images have been captured using a great variety of media. In the past two or three decades there has been a huge growth in the mass marketing of what might be considered generally as 'image capturing' equipment. Massive superstores are packed entirely with cameras, camcorders and other gadgets designed to produce better images, and to make it possible to manipulate photographic images on a computer - changing them, enhancing them and sending them by email across the world. By the time you read this there will no doubt be far more equipment available than is dealt with here.

In deciding what to include in your video life story, you might have images that were produced using processes and equipment that bear no resemblance to today's cameras and camcorders, possibly even dating back to the earliest days of photography around 150 years ago. Such media might include:

- Sepia prints - time has shown that these are often remarkably durable
- Black and white and/or colour prints - most people have lots of these and the prints will probably need sorting and labelling
- Transparencies
- Negatives
- Glass plates (glass negatives)

- Images on tinplates (positive)
- Black and white and/or colour cine film - this must be carefully stored and can be converted to video format
- Video recordings
- Digital camera stills
- Computer generated prints - if you have the skills and the software you can have a lot of fun compiling montages of photographs on a computer
- DVDs

In considering how to preserve your images it is important to remember that just because a medium is new it does necessarily stand a greater chance of surviving in perpetuity. Many families have in their possession photographs, often sepia, which are perhaps well over 100 years old but are still in good condition, despite little thought having been given to how they are stored. Some may even have been framed and hung on display and so have been exposed to the light for years. Compare that with the life expectancy of much stored computer media, about which little is known. It is suggested that CDs and DVDs might have a life expectancy of between 35 and 50 years, or less, even if stored in perfect conditions. For this reason, many experts consider that the best way to preserve an image is a photograph.

Another consideration is that with technological change comes obsolescence. Processes used to create and retrieve audio and visual items may not be available 100 years from now. It might even be necessary to transfer the material to more up-to-date media several times during your own lifetime. As usual, remember to leave instructions with your Gift to ensure that your material is transferred onto whatever modern systems might become available in the future.

To Sum Up

• There is a wide variety of equipment available for capturing images.

• Technological advances mean that processes and equipment used today may quickly become obsolete.

• Modern processes and equipment do not necessarily produce images that will last longer than those produced in the past.

• Many experts agree that the best way to ensure the durability of a still image is by photograph.

• You will need to leave instructions to ask future generations to transfer your material onto modern systems as they become available.

PART III

IF YOU ENJOY WRITING...

MY LIFE - AN AUTOBIOGRAPHY

Although the aim of this book is to encourage you to think of the variety of ways in which you can capture the essence of yourself without necessarily using the written word, if you enjoy writing and have a talent for using language there are a number of ways in which you can use this skill. How you choose to do this depends largely on the time you wish to devote to the project and what information you want to convey.

If you want to give future generations lots of detail about your life from birth until the present, you could consider writing a conventional autobiography. This will, of course, take a fair amount of time and organisation, but you might feel that the end result would be worth the effort.

If you are serious about this ambitious task you will need to organise yourself. If you simply start writing an account of your life from the day you were born and expect the story to flow over the pages, you are likely to be in for a disappointment! Apart from anything else, your memory will probably not oblige you by recalling everything in a neat and orderly fashion. You could be describing a special 10th birthday treat when a memory of your first day at school pops into your head.

Because your memory is likely to jump around all over the place, recalling different events at different times in your life, you will need to set up a system to help you collate all the information you want to include. A good idea would be to keep the information in a filing box as you gather it together. It should preferably be a box that is not too big and which has a handle, in case you want to carry it with you if you decide to go off somewhere to do some research. Such boxes are very cheaply available and will neatly house a set of envelope files which should be labelled clearly. If you decide to write your autobiography in purely chronological order, individual files should be labelled to indicate different periods such as 'Babyhood and the early years', 'School years', 'Going out to work' etc.

You should also get yourself a notebook that is small enough to fit into a handbag or pocket and try to get into the habit of always carrying it with you. You never know when you will have some time - perhaps on a train or while waiting for somebody - to think about your life and make notes about whatever comes into your head. Then you will be able to tear the pages out and file them in the appropriate place when you get home.

What Should You Include?

This is probably the most important decision you have to make about your autobiography. Because the purpose of writing it at all is to convey something of your life and times to your descendants, you will need to consider what aspects of life are important to you and make sure that these, and your personality, come through in your writing.

Remember that this is *your* story! Don't be too hesitant - grasp the nettle and show your enthusiasm for the things you love and your misgivings about the things you dislike. For example, in describing your school days you might choose to emphasise how unfair it was that a particular boy in the class was bullied and that the teachers seemed to be very ineffective in dealing with it. Or it could be that you felt disgruntled as a teenager when you had nowhere to go with your friends, so that you had to hang around on street corners. Perhaps you'd like to describe how unhappy you were that, when newly married, you had to move away from your home town because there was no reasonably priced accommodation and no work in the area where you had been brought up. Or how about describing your anger when your community lost part of its park to make way for a road expansion programme? Own your autobiography by infusing it with your own opinions and feelings about what is and was going on around you.

You might also like to describe something of the changes and events that occurred at different periods during your lifetime and how these affected you personally. Your descendants will be fascinated to hear about aspects of your life which are very different from theirs. Your own personal journey through life has run in tandem with some pretty exciting changes as the 20th century gave way to the 21st , so you are in a strong position to describe them 'from the inside'. Perhaps 'Brit pop', House music, Punk or 'Flower Power' coincided with your youth. Perhaps you were among the first women to give birth to a baby under water or to have your partner present at the birth. Perhaps your family had worked for generations in the same industry and it was during your lifetime that that particular industry declined and finally disappeared. Part VI of this book - This All Happened In My

Lifetime - will help you to think about such changes.

It goes without saying that you don't have to include everything you have ever done in your autobiography. That would hardly make a compelling read! If you are going to write a chronological account of your life, try to recall just a few events, places or people that typify what was happening to you during each particular episode. The trick is to help your descendants to stand in your shoes, to see life as you saw it. If your reader is able to feel your excitement, your fear, your sadness, he will never be bored.

Help From Others

As time passes, your filing box will be getting filled with notes about events, people and places you have recalled. When you feel you have exhausted your memory bank it will be time to talk to family members and old friends about experiences you have shared. You will be surprised how they can remind you of long-forgotten occasions. Don't be tempted, however, to talk to others about what you want to include in your autobiography before you have thoroughly searched your own memory, because the stories others tell you might well be slightly different from your recollections. Because your autobiography is *your* story it's always good to stand your ground and have confidence in your version of events unless, of course, you decide that you did have it wrong and can easily accept the other person's version.

Writing

Once you have collected as much material as you are satisfied with, you will need to think about how to put it together into a form that is structured and a good read. Whereas the information recorded up until now might have been noted as and when you've had the time, you will now need to be more disciplined and allocate regular time to the project.

The best approach is to structure writing time into your day on a regular basis. Try to make sure that when that time comes around you sit down to write even if you don't feel in the mood. Simply beginning to write can stimulate your thoughts. When the writing gets difficult it is surprising how you will welcome any little distraction, so, make yourself a cup of coffee, tell everyone that you do not want to be disturbed and switch on the answerphone system. Then just sit down and start!

Your first task will be to sort through all the material in your 'episode' envelopes to see if there is anything that you want to leave out. Do you really think this will be of interest to a reader in the future? What does it tell them about you and the times in which you are living? The fact that your best friend at school was called 'Jayne' will be of no interest - the sort of games you played together will be.

After you have decided what you want to include, take each episode, one at a time, and re-write each memory, adding detail and always making sure that the way you have written it reflects how you felt at the time.

When you are happy that your 'episode' files contain only those memories that you want to include, it will be time to consider writing the finished autobiography. The task will be made much easier if you have a computer, but if not you can use a typewriter or simply write by hand. It is not unknown for established and famous writers to hand-write their work as some people feel more closely connected with their work using a pen than using a computer.

Avoid an 'and then' approach which will simply read as a retrospective list of your activities:

'Each year we went to Brighton for a holiday. Mum would pack the cases and then Dad would put them into the boot of the car. Then we children would pile into the back seat and mum would ask if we had remembered to go to the toilet.'

Nothing here to hold the interest for long! A more interesting account might read:

Every year we went to Brighton for a holiday. Mum would pack the cases. The cases were dented and damaged from years of use and I had to share one with my sister. We'd pile the clothes up high and fight over the space in the case. Why I needed 20 t-shirts for a seven-day holiday I can't quite recall - at the time it made sense. I always suffered from car-sickness, and would feel sick even before we had started off. In the back of the car we'd sit, Mum dividing us in the hope of preventing us from arguing, but we would continually prod each other behind her back. We'd sit there for what seemed like hours waiting for Dad to do his last minute security checks around the house. The journey, only 23 miles, seemed to last a lifetime. After 10 minutes we demanded toilet breaks. 'I asked you if you wanted to go,' Mum would say. 'But I didn't want to go then,' would be our reply.

Such an account would probably have resonance for readers in the future.

While you are writing, try to let the language pour onto the page as if you were speaking. In that way it will appear natural. Something that slips naturally onto the page will slip naturally into the mind of the reader.

Although the suggestion was made at the beginning of this section that your autobiography would be an account of your life from birth to the present, do not think that you need to allocate equal space to each period, nor that you necessarily have to start at the beginning and move through your life chronologically. You will want to start off with something that grabs your reader's attention, and you may want to begin by writing about something that happened to you later in life. You can then introduce memories from an earlier time retrospectively. For example, if you write about your wedding day, you can reminisce about the fact that you were moving away from the house into which you were born and go on to describe childhood experiences. Or in describing one of the guests - an aunt with whom you used to spend holidays - you can paint a picture of early summer breaks on a farm in the country.

When you have completed your project up to the present you may decide to leave it at that, record the date on which it was finished, and take it to a local bookbinder to be turned into a hard-covered book with your name proudly embossed on the cover. On the other hand, your autobiography could be produced in loose-leaf format, using archival-quality paper slipped into archival-quality polyester sleeves and kept in a folder inside a box. This would leave you the option to update your story as your life takes interesting twists and turns in the future.

Whichever format you decide on, remember to include with it a simple family tree so that future generations can see where you fit into their family history.

To Sum Up

• Organise yourself - always carry a notebook so that you can jot down memories as they come to you.

• Begin to structure your work by using a filing system into which you can slip notes about episodes of your life.

• Describe your life from your own perspective - help the reader to stand in your shoes, to understand how events impacted on you.

• You don't need to recount events chronologically - make a strong start by introducing something powerful at the outset. You can then go back to reminisce about earlier events.

AN 'ALTERNATIVE' AUTOBIOGRAPHY

Perhaps you enjoy writing, but the idea of writing a full autobiography doesn't appeal to you. In that case you might prefer to produce a collection of writings about subjects that interest you. They could be funny or sad memories, significant things that have happened to you or any messages that you would like to convey to your descendants. Your writings could reflect your views about how change during your lifetime has affected you and your family, or might simply reflect your interests and hobbies. In this way you can convey something meaningful about your life and times to future generations without the rather onerous task of structuring events and happenings in your life, as you would in a 'conventional' autobiography.

What, then, would you like to write about? Consider some of the ideas that follow:

A Memorable Occasion

This description of a Sunday School outing in the North of England in the 1920s, shows how times have changed during the lifetime of Wyn Glover who is now in her 80s and lives in Manchester in the UK.

It was about 1925 when I joined a group of children for our Sunday School outing to the country - or so we thought. A coal delivery lorry arrived to collect us. Some benches were tied onto the back of it and we children all embarked and drove along the main road towards the 'country'. Unfortunately, we were on a main road where there was a tram track and, by some driving error, a tram hit the lorry, the insecurely-tied benches fell off, and all we screaming, bleeding children were disgorged into the roadway, just outside the entrance to the local cemetery. A funeral party was just emerging and the horrified mourners, seeing the mayhem, vacated their beautiful funeral coach and we were loaded into it and ferried to the nearby hospital. Nobody was badly hurt, just cuts and bruises, and we regarded that ride in the beautiful countryside as the best Sunday School treat ever!

Spirituality and Values

People vary considerably in the way they see and value different aspects of life and the world. Many autobiographies, while giving a detailed account of what a person did on a day-to-day basis, do not really convey anything about the subject's 'inner world' - what they valued, what things were really important to them, and what sustained them when life was tough.

You could take the opportunity in your 'alternative' autobiography to include something about those things that cause you to 'tingle'. In the 1980s, a popular BBC radio programme was called *The Tingle Factor*, where famous people were asked to discuss those things that made them 'tingle'. They usually included pieces of music and poetry, but you could also include a piece of prose or a favourite saying or photograph.

How you complete other parts of your Gift will say a lot about your values, but you might decide to say something more specifically here about your 'spiritual' life. It might even be that you consider this part of your life to be the most important, and that it will make up the entire contents of your Gift.

If you need a starting point, you might consider writing something about some of these questions:

- Do you believe in God?
- What does God mean to you?
- Does God play an important part in your day-to-day life?
- Do you believe in life after death?
- Do you belong to any particular religious group?
- What are the fundamental beliefs of your religion?
- What religious practices do you adhere to?
- Do you have a special place where you would like your ashes scattered?
- Do you consider yourself to be a 'spiritual' person and if so, what does that mean to you?
- Do you value family, friends and relationships above material possessions?
- Do you feel calm and content when you are in touch with the natural world?
- Is your personal 'inner journey' an important part of your life?
- If you feel you are on an 'inner journey' how has this progressed?
- What has helped you on your 'inner journey'?
- What personal qualities - such as honesty or loyalty - do you consider to be important? Why?
- Which of the people you have known have these qualities?

You might find it difficult to put your ideas about spirituality together and commit them to paper. If this is the case, another approach would be to make a collection of the writings by other people which you have found inspirational - perhaps some pieces from a religious book, a poem, or other writing. You could then copy your chosen writings onto archival-quality paper and take them along to a bookbinder to have them bound into a single volume. A very personal finishing touch would be to have a suitable title embossed on the front cover - something like: 'Inspirational Writings', 'Texts that have been Important to Me', or 'Pause for a Moment'. Add your name, and on the inside cover stick a simple family tree to identify who it was that compiled the volume.

By choosing writings that mean a lot to you and labelling them with a personal message, you will be creating a very meaningful and loving Gift for the Future, which could become an inspiration for a descendant.

Language

Words that have entered and left the language during your lifetime will say a lot about your life and times. For example, the word 'wireless' has left the English language probably because it is no longer an apt description of the artefact it originally described. In addition to such redundant words, there has been a huge influx of new words, many of them associated with new technologies. Computer, video and microwave are all examples of relatively new words used to describe new technological artefacts.

Jonathon Green's *Dictionary of New Words* is a good memory jogger if changes in language interest you (see Appendix 1).

Your Favourite Things

Here is your opportunity to record any of those things that make life worthwhile and which give you a buzz.

Most people have to spend a large amount of time simply earning a living. Some people are lucky enough to have sufficient capital not to have to go out to work, in which case they have much more choice about how to spend their time. For most people, however, varying degrees of choice have been involved in the job they do. For the musician, music might well be his favourite hobby; for the artist, his work is his life. But for most people, when work is finished they set about using their 'spare' time in a very wide variety of ways, which they hope to find fulfilling: football, theatre, gardening, music, meditation, cinema, bee-keeping, painting, reading, political activity, craft work, walking, mountaineering, cricket or sailing. Why not take the time here to tell future descendants what activities and pastimes really give you pleasure?

You could consider including the programme of your favourite football team or the catologue of the Horticultural Show in which you won first prize! Perhaps you'd even like to include an audio recording of yourself reading a favourite poem. Or imagine if, at some time in the future, a great-grandchild found that he or she shared with you a favourite piece of music!

What Makes You Angry?

What is it about modern life or people that makes you angry? Getting chewing gum stuck on your shoe, Third World debt, discrimination against minority groups, motorists who drive too fast? Has being angry ever got you into a tricky situation? Have you been involved in campaigning to change something that you do not like? Record your thoughts here.

Lovely Days

What about telling your descendants about some of the lovely days you have had? Ideally, they should be written soon after they have happened so that your memory is clear. There are obvious days you might like to include, such as your wedding day or the day you had your first child. But some lovely days come as a surprise: a day in the country or by the sea, a day when you visited your sister, or a day when you were given a surprise birthday treat.

The bonus of writing up lovely days is that they are kept fresh for you so that when you are old, with perhaps a failing memory, you can re-read and in a sense re-live those lovely days in their full glory!

Special People

You could include something about any person who is especially significant to you: a favourite aunt, a close friend, a 'guru'. It could be someone you have known through the years or someone with whom you had only a 'brief encounter'. What was it that made them special? In what circumstances did you meet? How did you part?

A Special Place

Cable Beach in Western Australia, the Grand Canyon, the garden at your granny's cottage in the country, or a buttercup-filled water meadow at Cambridge in England, might get a mention here. Describing your special place would say a lot about you, and who knows, it might have some resonance for a descendant at some time in the future.

What Marks You Out as Different?

As discussed earlier, geneticists have been building up a strong body of evidence in recent years which suggests that much of what you do and what you are is genetically pre-determined - the fact that you suffer badly from the cold for example, that you are a 'night owl', or that you are left-handed, have all been explained in terms of genetic predisposition.

One interesting anecdote tells of very unusual behaviour which was experienced by two men in the same family, two generations apart: while they slept they would jerk an arm into the air and allow it to crash down onto the face. The only difference was that one man had a large nose, which tended to get bruised by the action, while the other man had a smaller nose and suffered no damage. Can you imagine that such an odd habit could be passed down through the generations!

In addition to genetic influences, anyone who has first-hand experience of an adopted child will know that the environment in which a person is brought up plays a significant part in moulding their idiosyncrasies. It is uncanny that gestures and ways of walking or talking can somehow be 'picked-up' by a child from a parent, even when they do not share common genes.

The point is that to your descendants, your 'peculiarities' will be very interesting, particularly if they recognise them in themselves. So, if you are serious about passing on these little gems to future family members, include them in your Gift now!

Health and Well-Being

You may well at some time have been asked by a doctor, 'Is there a history of *such and such an illness* in your family?' Many people have no idea how to answer such a question. You can help to make questions like this easier for your descendants by telling them something of your general health and well-being, especially as this can have a bearing on their health.

If it is true that people enjoy talking about themselves, it is especially true that they enjoy talking about their health! As people get older they often fall into the habit of describing their physical frailties in detail to anyone who is prepared to listen - but that can be pretty boring! So, the golden rule here is: give any information that would be helpful to future generations, but don't indulge yourself by giving a blow by blow account of every ache and pain!

Medical knowledge and practice have been advancing rapidly during the past 100 years and continue to do so. Conditions that would have killed people during the middle years of the 20th century are now treatable or even curable. How much will medical knowledge have advanced in the future, and what conditions for which the prognosis is currently very bleak will be curable?

Your descendants will be very interested to know something about how your health problems were treated - either by yourself informally or by the medical practitioners of the day. Perhaps you found a way of managing your migraine or irritable bowel syndrome. Diet might have helped. Do you eat your five portions of fruit and vegetables every day? If you use alternative therapies, such as homeopathy or reflexology, then you may like to say something about that too.

A story recalled by one lady in her 80s shows how medical services in the UK have changed since the early decades of the 20th century:

In the days prior to the National Health Service you had to pay three shillings and six pence (17p) to visit the doctor and five shillings (25p) if he visited you at home. Shortage of money usually meant you had to be desperate to consult a doctor! One particular incident I will always remember. The rag and bone man (who used to collect anything people didn't want) used to come round the streets collecting empty jam jars and rewarding the givers (mostly children) with a balloon in exchange. My cousin Doris, who lived nearby, came with such a jar but she tripped and fell and the broken jar severed an artery in her wrist. My mother rushed out, tore up an old sheet and sent me to collect her mother. Very few people had telephones in those days and there were very few public phone boxes and no '999' calls, so the two women then had to walk to the tram stop to wait for a tram to take Doris to the nearest hospital, where she was duly stitched up. I don't know how much they had to pay for that.

Your Least Favourite Things

Most people wouldn't have too much difficulty in filling this space! Being stuck in traffic, road rage, automated messages whilst being kept on hold on the phone, chemicals in food... the list goes on! Can you imagine what things irritated your great-grandparents? Was it the fact that the man who toured the streets to light the gas lamps sang loudly or that the man selling fish would always set up his stall in a way that obstructed the footpath? Would you believe that as early as the 1920s there were complaints about traffic congestion in central London! Personal dislikes that seem obvious to us now will be an interesting insight into early 21st century life for our descendants.

Money and Prices in Your Lifetime

Perhaps you'd be interested to know just how much your great-grandparents paid for a pair of shoes - if they could afford to buy them. Or how much it cost to buy a loaf of bread. To make sense of the cost we would also need to know how much they earned, so if you include a section on prices be sure to say something about your earnings too. Alternatively, it has been suggested that quoting the current price of a Mars Bar is a useful way of helping someone in the future to understand today's prices. This, of course, assumes that Mars bars are still around in hundreds of years time!

Things You Would Like to Have Done

Perhaps you have some regrets about the job you do and would have loved to have become an actor, a show jumper or a landscape gardener. Perhaps you would have liked to travel more, to have learned to drive or fly, or to have moved to the country. Perhaps thinking about these things now will inspire you to change the course of your life. Here is the place to air your fantasies and dreams.

How You Have Changed

If you are interested in your personality, hang-ups or anxieties, you might like to say something about how you have developed and changed during your lifetime. Perhaps you have worked on being more assertive or less of a control freak. Perhaps a traumatic experience like a serious road accident changed you. Or maybe someone you met changed your direction.

Favourite Food and Recipes

Here is your chance to share your thoughts on food and cooking. It's surprising how very different people are in their attitudes to food - for some people it is one of life's major pleasures, while for others it is a chore to get through and they would prefer to live off a supply of nutritional tablets! Perhaps you are a vegetarian or vegan? There might also be some family recipes passed down from your granny, which will be guaranteed not to get lost if you include them in your Gift. Your favourite 'tipple' could also get a mention.

Clothes

You only have to look back to the last decade to see that fashions in clothing change very rapidly. Can you imagine what people will be wearing 100 years from now? Don't you think your descendants will be interested to know what you were wearing?

An interesting snippet to include could be something about your favourite items of clothing - perhaps an outfit you had for a special occasion or simply something you feel comfortable sitting around the house in. Babies' clothes would be interesting too because they have changed almost beyond recognition in the past couple of decades, with white and pastel colours giving way to bright colours and adult styles. Children's fashion designers seem to be reverting back to the 19th century and earlier, when children were seen as small adults and were dressed as such.

Of course, jeans have been the universal fashion item of the second half of the 20th century for men, women and children. Jeans could be seen as *the* fashion item that symbolises the last decades of the 20th century. However, designers have been clever in producing new styles in jeans from season to season - flared or straight, hipsters or waist fitting, 'drain pipes' or loose fitting, bootleg or twisted - to ensure that consumers continually bought new pairs.

To Sum Up

• If you enjoy writing but don't want to tackle a conventional autobiography, simply make a collection of writings.

• Include anything that interests you about your life and the world you inhabit.

WORDS CAN SAY SO MUCH

Don't you think that the following pieces of writing would say a great deal if they were included as part of an alternative autobiography?

The first describes a lesson learned through the letters of a grandmother and is taken from Julia Cameron's inspiring book, *The Artist's Way*. She illustrates the value of paying attention to the moment:

'Flora and fauna reports,' I used to call the long, winding letters from my grandmother. 'The forsythia is starting and this morning I saw my first robin... the roses are holding their own in spite of the heat... my Christmas cactus is getting ready...'

Life through grandma's eyes was a series of small miracles: the wild tiger lilies under the cottonwoods in June; the quick lizard scooting under the gray river rock she admired for its satiny finish. Her letters clocked the seasons of the year and her life. She lived until she was eighty, and the letters came until the very end. When she died, it was as suddenly as her Christmas cactus: here today, gone tomorrow. She left behind her letters and her husband of sixty-two years. Her husband, my grandfather Daddy Howard, an elegant rascal with a gambler's smile and a loser's luck, had made and lost several fortunes, the last of them permanently. He drank them away, gambled them away, tossed them away the way she threw crumbs to her birds. He squandered life's big chances the way she savoured the small ones. 'That man,' my mother would say.

My grandmother lived with that man in tiled Spanish houses, in trailers, in a tiny cabin halfway up a mountain, in a railroad flat, and finally, in a house made out of ticky-tacky where they all looked just the same. 'I don't know how she stands it,' my mother would say, furious with my grandfather for some new misadventure. She meant she didn't know why. The truth is we all knew how she stood it. She stood it by standing knee-deep in the flow of life and paying close attention.

My grandmother was gone before I learned the lesson her letters were teaching: survival lies in sanity, and sanity lies in paying attention... the tiger lilies are blooming, the lizard has found that spot of sun, the roses are holding despite the heat.

My grandmother knew what a painful life had taught her: success or failure, the truth of a life really has little to do with its quality. The quality of life is in proportion, always, to the capacity for delight. The capacity for delight is the gift of paying attention.

In the following piece of writing, music is used to describe a lifetime spent in England and Canada and describes events during the second half of the 20th century. In just a couple of hours, Julia was able to produce something that will be of great interest to her descendants. Not only does it describe the emotions evoked by music at different times and in different places, but it also describes changes in the technology of music production during the early to middle years of her life. Broad technological change is cleverly intertwined with very personal moments.

A personal account written by Julia, born in England in 1955, emigrated to Canada 1980

One of my most humiliating and very early memories of school is from music class. The children were split into Singers and Learners and each group had its own set of benches positioned at opposite sides of the classroom. Presumably the good Singers had the difficult sections of the songs and the Learners the more manageable parts - I don't recall. But I do remember the one lesson when I inadvertently went to the wrong side and stood on the Singers' bench. We started to sing, but after a few bars my out-of-tune drone must have been clearly audible because the teacher stopped the song and, in front of the whole class, I had to walk across to the other side and take up my proper place with the Learners.

I have been learning about music ever since. As I sit here now, on the far side of 45 and on the far side of the Atlantic from that classroom scene, it seems to me that music is one of the most powerful ways to recall events, people and places in my life. And over time I have re-evaluated and come to love music that I had dismissed years earlier.

Earliest musical memories growing up in England are of the radio (then often called the 'wireless'). The vocal group on *Sing Something Simple* comes to mind - I think it was on Sunday evenings.

We had a record player too, on which mum played her Frank Sinatra long-playing records (LPs). For some time I dismissed Frank Sinatra as someone boring from my parents' generation, until one day, not too long ago, I really listened to 'In the Wee Small Hours of the Morning' and recognised it as an absolute masterpiece. It now gives me the dual pleasure of remembering my home and my parents, and appreciating the intrinsic beauty of those wistful love songs.

We had a few LPs but most of our records were just 'singles'. Usually on a Saturday Dad would go into town and buy a new one; this was before we had a car, but sometimes he took me on the back of his motorbike. I would have been seven or eight years old and had my own crash helmet. This was the early 60s - the beginning of that amazing era of the Beatles, the Stones and The Who, but our house resonated with such eclectic choices as 'Does Your Chewing Gum Lose its Flavour on the Bedpost Overnight?' and 'Big Bad John', which still make me smile and think of my Dad. Thus it was that I had only the radio for listening to the Beatles and the rest.

Growing up involved boys and since, by 1966, I was at an all-girls grammar school, my only contact with them was through church and 'Youth Club'. Today, all it takes is the first few bars of The Archies, 'Honey... Oh Sugar Sugar' and I am 14 again at the Youth Club dance in my sleeveless polo-neck and mini-skirt.

A little older now - the summer of 1971. I was 16, O-levels all done and I was hooked on Leonard Cohen. Joni Mitchell and Judy Collins were right there with him. I had a group of friends and I actually had a boyfriend. I really had a crush on his friend Simon who was crazy about Judy Collins. It is Simon I remember most clearly whenever I hear her version of 'I Loved You in the Morning'. Dishy Simon is probably chubby and grey by now, but Judy Collins' voice on my CD player is as clear and pure as ever. But back then everything was still vinyl with those gorgeous album covers.

My sister, two years younger, had different friends and different tastes in music, but we shared a room and pooled our pocket money to get our own record player. According to her, the only factor in deciding which one to get was that it had to have 'sliders' instead of knobs. So, regardless of acoustic quality, we ended up with a white record player with sliders to control the volume. She had the single of The Temptations' 'Just my Imagination', and used to set the record player to repeat and play it over and over. It says something about that song that I never tired of it, and hearing it today I always think of my sister and miss her, and wish I lived closer.

Cassette tapes must have come along not too long afterwards because that is how I remember the music when I left home and headed to London University in 1973. My first year all-girls Hall of Residence was named Nutford House, so Tina Turner's 'Nutbush City Limits' became a theme song for us in the heady year of discos and discovery. And as I hear, in my head, Tina belting out, 'They called it NUTBUSH...' I can see all those girls I befriended and remember one of the best years of my life.

In my second year at University I fell in love with a guy who introduced me to a whole new world of music - Jefferson Airplane, The Doors, Neil Young and that whole incredible West Coast Psychedelic sound. We married in 1978, moved to London, Ontario, in 1980 and split up in 1982. Ironically, his favourite song was 'Happy Together' by The Turtles and I think of him when I hear that song and I remember the good times. I still have some of the tapes that he made me, brittle with age after 20 years but with too many memories to throw away.

So I was in Canada - the homeland of some of my teenage idols, Leonard Cohen, Joni Mitchell and Neil Young. I was disappointed to discover that Leonard was a much bigger name in the UK and Europe than in his native land, and that many Canadians had not even heard of him. By 1985 I was remarried to a Canadian who introduced me to Gordon Lightfoot's folksy commentaries and Harry Chaplin's poignant 'Cat's In the Cradle'. My music collection grew a little more.

In 1993 I was transferred out west to Calgary, home of the Calgary Stampede, cowboys and country music. In the UK and Eastern Canada I had dismissed country out of hand. But, a friend got us free tickets to an Alan Jackson concert and I enjoyed it immensely. If you can't beat 'em, open your mind and join 'em. So country music, admittedly in small doses, joined my collection.

By now, of course, CDs were the new media. Touted then as indestructible although we all know differently now, it was easy to fit a lot of music into a smaller space. This is just as well because my next foray was into classical music and my CD collection was about to grow exponentially as a result.

At the time, I car pooled[2] with a wonderful friend and one day we had the radio tuned to the classical station. I was infuriated that I recognised the music from some long-ago classical music class at school, but could not remember the name of the piece or the composer (it turned out to be Holst's 'Planet Suite'). Always up for a challenge, I embarked on a mission to understand classical music. It actually became a joint project with my car-pool friend as we discovered the wonders of classical music

---

[2] This was a term that described the custom of car sharing which emerged towards the end of the 20th century largely as a response to claims that too much car usage was causing environmental damage and bringing about global warming.

and bought season tickets to the Calgary Philharmonic and tons of CDs. Listening to music written so many years ago does not remind me of one individual, like most of the contemporary music I like. Rather it connects me to the generations of unknown people, some of them my ancestors, who have listened to and loved the same music.

Fast forward to today, 2002. I have two beautiful daughters of my own who can burn CDs and download MP3 files at the click of a mouse. They do not even need to leave the house to get new music. I remember my sister and I trying to learn all the words of The Kinks' 'Lola'. We would rush to the radio whenever it came on and scribble down a few more of the lyrics every time - '...tastes just like Cherry c-o-o-l-a'. It took us weeks, I am sure, to get the whole thing on paper so we could finally sing it together in our equally out-of-tune voices. Today my girls can use a search engine and get the lyrics from the web with a few mouse clicks. Way more efficient, but so much less fun!

As we speak I am on a nostalgia kick with my music. Through the wonders of email and instant messaging I've been back in touch with old friends from England, who have reminded me once more of some of the wonderful old music of my youth. I am busy filling gaps in my collection with Van Morrison, Bob Seger, Pink Floyd and whoever else takes my breath away for a few seconds and makes me glad to be alive.

So this brings me full circle. Forty years ago I was ashamed, but now I am exceedingly thankful, that I accepted my rightful spot on that bench as a Learner. I think those self-confident, knowledgeable, good Singers have missed out on something. I acknowledge that I needed to learn about music and it took me on a journey throughout my life. It feels to me now like the music and the people who showed it to me are inextricably blended into a beautiful harmony that I can hum in my head whenever I wish.

PART IV

SOME MORE IDEAS

JUST PICK 'N' MIX

Only you know what it is about yourself and your life and times that you would like to preserve and communicate to your descendants; this will largely determine the form your Gift will take.

So, how *do* you want to communicate with the future? So far we have given thought to the conventional ways of recording your life - by words and pictures. We have considered:

- A photo album
- A video recording
- A conventional autobiography
- A pot-pourri of writings about you and your life and times - which you could consider as an 'alternative' to an autobiography
- A collection of inspirational writings

Now you are ready to think about other options. You could consider including:

- An audio recording
- A Treasure Box
- A letter
- Completed *Factual Information Sheets*
- Completed *Thoughts & Feelings Information Sheets*

- A scrapbook/Life Book
- A collage
- A journal/diary
- A family tree
- A timeline
- A piece of reportage

Why not combine some of these ideas? For example, if time is limited, you might feel that what you want to convey can easily be communicated by completing the *Factual Information Sheets*, templates for which are provided at the back of this book, and supplementing these with a small photo album of your life. If you like the idea of producing a Treasure Box you could include in it a family tree, a small photo album and/or a letter. A Life Book could include a family tree and/or a timeline.

Alternatively, you might choose simply to compile a collection of your favourite poems, prose and inspirational writings and include a family tree to identify yourself, with an introductory note saying something about your spiritual life. If this was bound and given a suitable title it would make a very impressive Gift. A simple, small photo album of your life could be accompanied by a comprehensive family tree.

The possibilities are endless - so go for it and pick 'n' mix. The result could be very exciting.

The point about these guidelines is that they are simply suggestions for different forms your Gift could take, and there is no need for them to be mutually exclusive. Only you know what aspects of your life and times you would like to record for your descendants and how you would like your Gift to look. Have confidence - make a Gift that truly reflects your individuality.

To Sum Up

• The form your Gift takes will be largely determined by what you want to convey.

• Your Gift can be a single item or a package incorporating more than one idea.

• Read these guidelines, but then make your Gift your own creation.

A LETTER

There is something very personal and somehow romantic about this method of communicating with the future. If you have ever read a letter from a soldier at the front line to a loved one back home you will know just how intimate and revealing it can be. Even something written in less difficult times, perhaps a postcard sent from the seaside or a greetings card with only a few words, seems to say so much about the writer.

You could use a computer to write your letter or, if you feel more comfortable writing by hand, and have lots of time and patience, you might like to produce a hand-written letter. This would be especially appropriate if you have splendid handwriting. The works produced by monks before the advent of printing come to mind. If you choose to do this you could mention that your method of presentation is not typical of life in the early 21st century.

You can be sure that a hand-written letter would feel very personal to a descendant in years to come. It has been said that you can tell a lot about a person from their handwriting - whether the writing, and the writer, is bold and quick or gentle and ponderous, careful and fussy or erratic and messy. It's also surprising how handwriting styles can pass from generation to generation - time and again people say that their handwriting very much resembles that of a parent.

A letter is a very direct means of communication. You can personally address your descendants and feel as if you are speaking to them. Try to let the thoughts flow and be unrestrained in what you say. You would surely feel a tingle if you were able to read a letter written by a great-grandparent or some other ancestor, particularly if it was addressed especially to you.

Remember, it will help to show who the letter was written by if you keep with it a simple family tree identifying yourself within the family.

You may well have in your possession some old letters (perhaps written by a grandparent) that you would like to preserve and include in your Gift. If so, but you find that they are fading, it would be worthwhile typing a copy of them, printing them on acid-free paper and storing them along with the originals. By doing so you will ensure that when the originals fade, at least the content of what was written will be preserved.

Content

Before you begin your letter you will have to decide to whom you would like to address it. There are a number of alternatives here. You can write an 'open' letter which is simply addressed to any descendant at any time in the future, or you can address it to a particular person - in the example below the letter is addressed to a grandchild. The letter can be written as and when the fancy takes you, or it can mark a special occasion - perhaps a baby's birth or a wedding.

Some autobiographical material could be included in the letter or you might choose simply to pass on some loving words, perhaps about lessons you have learned and things you have enjoyed in life. You might like to include some of the topics and ideas discussed in the section on making an audio recording. Or you might like to make the letter a spontaneous flow of your thoughts.

The following example might help to get you started:

A Letter to a Grandchild

If you have recently had (or are about to have) a new grandchild, you will perhaps feel moved to write - possibly on the day he or she was born, or soon after.

THIS LETTER WAS WRITTEN BY (Name) ON (Full Date)

To my dear new grand-daughter (name not yet chosen),

It is now 11pm on Wednesday 20th November 2001. I would like to tell you something of the happenings of the day and about our family and the world on the day you were born.

Your birth

You came into the world today! Max, your father, phoned me on his mobile phone late last night to say that he had just taken Jane, your mother, into hospital. Mobile phones have only been in general use for about the past 10 years and they are very useful for such occasions. I was so excited I could hardly sleep, but must have dropped off at some point because I was awakened at 7.15 this morning when Max phoned us to say that labour was well under way and that he would let us know when you were born. Then there was a telephone call from Marilyn (Jane's mother) to ask if we had any news. She lives in New York so must have felt terrible being too far away to be of much help. What a long day of waiting it was - at 6pm Max phoned to say you had arrived at 4.30 pm after quite a difficult birth, but that both mother and baby were doing well.

The evening was taken up with me phoning family and friends with the news of your arrival. I have to say that you were a very much wanted and welcome baby. Just as I was getting ready for bed - around 11pm - Max phoned to say he had returned home and was sitting on the floor in the kitchen, sipping a glass of wine, and that he couldn't stop smiling. He said you were a very good-looking baby and that you seemed to have inherited your mother's build because you were quite long and slim. He also said that you appeared to be very placid and keen on your food, because you were already feeding well. He promised to email us some pictures of you he had taken with his 'digital' camera soon after you were born. Such cameras have only recently become widely available and, for the first time, we do not need to use a 'film' in the camera. The pictures can be loaded onto a computer and printed out or even sent to someone else by email - how clever!

Your parents

Max was 33 and Jane 28 when they met on the cruise liner on which they were both working in the summer of 1999. They had both taken time out from their teaching jobs and were enjoying travelling the world on a luxury liner. Jane was working in the nursery and Max was a barman. Soon after they met they returned to live in a flat in Perth, Western Australia, and continued with their teaching careers. They married in the summer of 2000 at the local Catholic Church.

Max and Jane are a lovely match. She is energetic and dynamic, often plunging into new projects, but Max counters this by being a little more laid back and circumspect. They both enjoy the outdoor life and regularly go for long walks in the bush. They know every shrub, plant and tree for miles around! A favourite holiday destination is Bali and they are both good surfers.

What I was doing today

Your grandfather (Peter) and I are now retired, although we both still do a little part-time work. I, like your parents, am a teacher and do occasional teaching when I am needed. Before he retired last year, Peter was a consultant civil engineer. Today, being Wednesday, I went for my computer training at a local adult education centre. We have both finished the modules on word processing and are now working on a module called 'Webwise'. We have bought a computer for home and are linked to the Internet. Peter is much more adept at using the computer than I am. We both like to keep up to date with modern communications technology and feel very excited by the wealth of information we can access via the 'Web'. We can even send emails to friends in the USA and the UK. Until recently, we could only telephone them or write a letter that took several days to be delivered. Nowadays, people refer to the mail service as 'snail-mail'.

In the future we believe we might spend one day a week looking after you as Jane is planning to return to work. We are very much looking forward to that.

A wish for the future

I think I will end this letter with a wish for you and your life. Your early photographs emailed by Max show you as a very peaceful baby. And so, I wish you a life of inner peace. I believe that love and happiness do not come from external possessions but from within the self. With inner peace and love you will be able to journey through life, developing your talents and savouring the rich joys and treasures that life offers you. I look forward to getting to know you.

With much love,

(Signature and Full Name)

To Sum Up

- A letter:
  - is a very personal way of communicating with the future
  - can be written on a computer or by hand
  - can be addressed to a particular person or can be written for any reader
  - can be written on a special occasion, such as a birth or wedding, or just when the fancy takes you.
- The content can include anything - details of your personal life, messages to future generations, or events in the wider world.
- Ensure durability by following the rules of good conservation - use archival-quality materials and store in a stable environment.
- To make your identity clear keep a simple family tree with the letter.

A TREASURE BOX

Wow! This is where you can really have some fun.

Anyone who has had the sad and poignant task of clearing a house after someone has died knows that everyone collects, to a greater or lesser degree, artefacts that have significance for them. House clearing is indeed an occasion that demonstrates that one person's treasure is another person's rubbish.

However, if you could use some foresight now and collect in one place a selected variety of your much loved and highly valued possessions, you can lead your descendants directly to your treasure. You will have saved them the difficult task of sifting through your possessions and having to decide what to keep and what to discard.

A Treasure Box filled with your carefully chosen artefacts, records, writings and possessions would certainly make a truly meaningful Gift.

Those treasures you have chosen to keep and have then selected for inclusion in your Gift will, of course, say a great deal about you. If your Infant School reports are included it is guaranteed that you (and your parents) were very methodical. It takes a lot of organisation to keep school reports safe for a lifetime! If you have your children's first teeth, carefully wrapped in tissue paper and stored in a velvet-lined box, this would suggest you have a somewhat sentimental streak. The same would apply to anyone who has kept greetings cards over the years.

How durable would you like your Treasure Box to be? Would you be happy if it lasted until the end of the 21st century - so that it could be seen by your great-great-grandchildren? Of course nothing lasts forever, but if you are prepared to spend a little time and money you can take steps to ensure that you slow down the deterioration process and maximise its chances of surviving for a long time.

First you will need to think about the kind of box you use. The best option would be to use one made of stainless steel, which is the material recommended for time capsules, but which is unlikely to be available in the size and shape you want. You might also think that it is not very attractive. If you go for wood, which would be attractive to keep on display, try to find a box that is solid and old. New wood gives off gases, and this is especially true of MDF because the adhesives used during the production process contain harmful chemicals. Another good alternative would be to use one of the specially made archival-quality, strong cardboard boxes that are made of acid-free board and have reinforced metal corners. Unfortunately, these are not particularly attractive to look at but you could decorate it.

An important factor to bear in mind when you are selecting items for your Treasure Box is how long they will last. You might think that a pot of dehydrated noodles or some other processed food would say a lot about the time in which you are living, but do not include any food in your Gift - it will deteriorate very quickly. The possible durability of particular items is something that your local museum conservator will be able to help you with. You might also like to discuss with him or her the box you are using and any other questions about storing your collection.

The treasures you include could back-up what you have written if you decide to complete the *Information Sheets* or they could complement what you have recorded in your conventional or 'alternative' autobiography. Or, with a few explanatory notes, the Treasure Box will stand alone, saying a great deal about you.

For many people the problem is going to be what *not* to include. The Treasure Box can easily turn into a Treasure Chest! It is unlikely that your descendants will want to keep a huge pile of your 'treasures' because they will, of course, go through life collecting their own. A whole box of baby teeth, for example, even if it takes up only a little space, would not be of much interest. After all, one person's baby tooth is much like another! Bear in mind that a smaller number of well-stored, and thus well-preserved, attractive artefacts will prove more informative than a mass of knick-knacks.

A novel way of preserving something for your Treasure Box would be to encase it in resin. You can buy a resin kit which allows you to pour liquid resin over whatever it is you want to preserve - perhaps a flower from your wedding bouquet or a decoration from a cake. When the resin sets hard you can then sand it and buff it until it is clear like glass. It can even be used as a paperweight or an ornament.

Making up a Treasure Box would not be too time-consuming and it can be added to whenever you come across an interesting item that passes the following three tests:

1. Is this object important to me?

2. Does it convey something to my descendants about me/my life/my family?

3. Will the item stand the test of time?

As a starting point you might consider including in your Treasure Box:

- A school report
- A small collection of photographs taken at different times in your life with explanatory captions
- Some greetings cards - perhaps ones received when you moved house, married or had a baby
- An ornament from your wedding cake
- A piece of jewellery - perhaps an engagement ring
- Some letters
- Birth, marriage or death certificates
- A cassette recording made by yourself
- A video recording showing aspects of your life and times
- Any newspaper cuttings that might be of special interest
- Any small artefacts that you feel say something about the period in which you are living
- The programme of a theatrical production in which you appeared or the catalogue of a gardening show in which you won first prize
- A commemorative programme of some kind, for example, a centenary celebration or visit of a famous person
- A small book
- A collection of writings

If you keep your box on display this will remind you to add significant artefacts as they come to hand.

It can't be emphasised too much that you must be very selective with the items that you include and that the box must be small and well labelled. You could also add an explanatory note about the contents. It could be that perhaps after your death, other family members might like to add something to your Treasure Box - perhaps something they would like to write about you. Do you believe that your descendants would be happy - and proud - to keep your box, if it is attractive and not much bigger than say, a shoebox? Would you like your Treasure Box to be used occasionally as a talking point? You can be sure that anything that is too big to display easily would almost certainly be packed away at the back of a cupboard or attic and perhaps eventually thrown away.

You might be tempted to line the box with fabric - don't! The lining will be at risk from insect infestation. You should also bear in mind when putting your Treasure Box together that some materials give off gasses that can lead to the deterioration of things with which they are stored. For example, if something made of wool is stored near silver, the silver will very soon turn black as a result of the sulphur given off by the wool. Newspapers or other inferior quality papers will also contaminate the other contents of your box. You can prevent this by separating the items and storing them in suitable polyester envelopes.

Finally, if you decide to protect the contents of your box with bubble wrap or tissue paper, make sure that it is archival quality.

To Sum Up

• What you choose to include in your Treasure Box will say a lot about you without you necessarily writing a single word, although you might choose to include some written material in your package.

• Remember to add an explanatory note to your Treasure Box, explaining the contents.

• Include only those things that pass the three tests: they are significant to you, they will convey something important about you and your times to future generations, and they are durable.

• If your Treasure Box is attractive it will be kept on display and will stand less chance of being lost.

• Pay attention to the type of box you use and take steps to keep the contents in good condition. Consult your local museum conservator for advice.

• As always, include a simple family tree to identify who you are.

A COLLAGE

If you have artistic flair, an interesting way of communicating something about yourself, your life and the world in which you are living would be to make a collage which could then be framed. In the past it was common for women to make cross-stitch designs in celebration of occasions such as a wedding or a birth. These would then be framed and presented as gifts to mark the event. Such mementos took pride of place in many homes. In some communities women would get together to make a quilt or wall hanging to mark a special occasion - perhaps the most famous example is the Bayeux tapestry in France, which depicts the invasion of Britain by William the Conqueror. It is a very grand example of how stitching can tell a story without a word being used!

What Materials to Include

Embroidery, cross-stitch, lace making, and all sorts of different textile techniques could be used to create a visually attractive and unusual Gift for future generations. Of course, the term 'collage' can be very widely interpreted here and you could choose from any of a number of materials and artefacts such as:

- One or two photographs of yourself, perhaps showing you as a baby and then as an adult
- A photograph of your family group
- A photograph of your home

- A photograph of a much-loved place
- Pieces of fabric from a favourite, now worn-out and reluctantly discarded dress
- Newspaper cuttings
- A postcard
- A piece of hair, perhaps with a ribbon
- A programme of a much-loved event or exhibition
- Any item that represents a favourite hobby - a football programme, a picture of a garden, a photograph of you riding a horse

How to Display the Work

You could display the work on either paper or board (acid-free, of course) or on fabric. Once you have arranged the component parts you could decorate the work. If you enjoy sewing you might embellish the collage with some embroidery motifs. If you paint or draw you could decorate the mounting board artistically, using paints or pastels. If you enjoy the great outdoors you might like to have a background of trees and the countryside. Or a gardener might choose to include lots of pictures of flowers - or even some pressed flowers.

Remember, as always, to help your descendants see how you fit into the family history by labelling the back of the frame carefully with your name, and attaching a simple family tree identifying yourself. You might also include your name as part of the collage itself.

If you like the idea of depicting your life and times with a collage but don't feel you have the time or ability, you might find a local artist who could take on the task for you. Alternatively, in some areas, workshops are held to help and encourage you to make a 'Memories' collage. You can find information about this in Appendix 2.

To Sum Up

- A framed picture or collage is a very creative way of recording the essence of your life and times.
- A wide variety of materials can be used to artistic effect.

A JOURNAL

Perhaps you already keep a journal. If so, have you ever considered why you do that? Perhaps you think that at some time in the future you would like to look back and remind yourself of what you were doing in past years. Or perhaps you see writing a journal as a kind of therapy - a way of getting something off your chest at the end of a busy day. It's true that for many people writing something down is a good way of off-loading, like letting off steam by writing a letter to someone with whom you feel very angry, and then throwing the letter away. Or it might be that you see your journal as an account of your life which you would like to preserve so that someone can read about you in the future.

If the latter is the case then it is worth spending a little time thinking about what you record as well as making sure that the materials of which your journal is made will stand the passing of the years.

What to Include

The first point to make is that there is nothing to stop you from writing more than one journal - apart from a shortage of time of course! In that way you could perhaps keep one journal to remind yourself of what you have done and to get things off your chest, and another journal as your 'Gift for the Future'.

If you intend your journals to be read by people in the future this will almost certainly influence what you record. Some of the day-to-day goings on, possibly of interest to you when you come to look back over your life, would probably be rather tedious to people in the future. Take, for example, the excitement of what used to be called 'dating' and 'going to the pictures'. The names of who you were dating and where you went on your dates will probably be interesting for you to look back on, but your descendants reading your journal in say, 50 years time, would be more interested in the social conventions of 'dating' in your time and of the mechanics of 'going to the pictures'. Within the last 50 years, for example, 'dating' language has changed considerably. The terms 'walking out with' and 'courting' now bring a smile to the face and have given way to 'dating' and being 'an item'. Many people now talk of going to the 'movies' rather than the 'pictures' and the ornate cinemas of 50 years ago, with usherettes and pitch darkness, have given way to swish emporiums of smooth lines, more light and hence no one to show you to your seat. The programme, instead of the 'A' and 'B' films of bygone years coupled with Pathé Pictorial news, is usually one film supported by trailers and advertisements which have become art in themselves.

In a nutshell, your descendants will be more interested in your reflections on aspects of the world in which you are living than in the name of your boyfriend or the fact that you had an argument about which film to see. When writing a journal for future generations always have an eye to your audience.

Your descendants would like to see the world of days gone by through your eyes. For example, you're having difficulties coming to terms with the new information technology system that has been installed at work. A candid, day-by-day account of how you deal with that would be interesting. Or maybe you are about to have a baby and have read and received a variety of conflicting advice about how to care for your baby. Fashions in child care change with each generation so an explanation of which you choose to follow would make fascinating reading. These are the issues and challenges that pepper modern life and which preoccupied you at particular times in your life. It might be that they were a minor concern or perhaps they caused you many sleepless nights. Your account of them will make interesting and intriguing reading for your descendants and it might well be that much of what you write will have resonance for them.

If you carry your diary with you in a handbag or pocket it is quite likely to become dog-eared and tattered by the end of each year. If you intend it to be readable for future generations you could think about keeping your diary at home where it will be less likely to get damaged.

Finally, remember the good rules of preservation when writing your journal and to use archival-quality paper.

To Sum Up

• If you keep a journal, think about why you are doing so.

• If it is to preserve something of your life and times for future generations consider whether what you are writing will be of interest to them.

• If necessary you could keep more than one journal.

• Try to keep your journal in a place where it will not get damaged.

A LIFE BOOK

Instead of producing a single photo album of your life and times, you might decide to broaden the contents and include items other than photographs and thus broaden your album into a 'Life Book'.

Obvious items for inclusion are greetings cards. Many people, after birthdays or other anniversaries, tuck away, in a drawer somewhere, beautiful cards containing loving messages. The progress of their lives is chronicled by occasions such as birthdays, an engagement, a wedding, illnesses, bereavements. The extent to which people send greetings cards varies considerably - some countries have a long history of card sending going back a 100 years, while in others the idea is relatively new. Even in countries where there is a strong tradition of sending cards some people and some families are more tuned in to sending cards than others.

A collection of newspaper cuttings is a very easy and effective way of recording events during your lifetime - whether the cuttings are of international or more local events. Man's first step on the Moon, the Mayor presenting you with an award at your school prize day, or the chairman of your company giving you a gold watch on your retirement, could all be chronicled using cuttings from national and local newspapers.

Other possible items for inclusion in a Life Book could be concert or show tickets and programmes, birth, marriage and death certificates, anything, in fact, that you might include in a Treasure Box but which is flat enough to mount in an album!

How then do you go about producing a Life Book that reflects you and your life and times?

Selecting Items

Some people hoard lots of things and turn this into a hobby by saying that they are 'collecting' different artefacts. The trick is to decide which of the possessions you have accumulated will be of interest in the future. For inclusion in a Life Book they must obviously be flat - if they are not flat they could be included in a Treasure Box. It is important that the items selected are very personal to you and say something about you. Extra interest will be added if they are items that have either become obsolete or have considerably changed. A good example of this would be an early sports programme showing players wearing old-fashioned kit. Anyone who has a greetings card or postcard from the early 20th century knows that fashions in these change considerably over time so these also would be of interest.

Presentation and Layout

Once you have decided which items to include and how to best preserve them, the fun begins and you can go to town on how you lay out each page.

Put the photographs and other memorabilia in date order and decide which will go on each page. Juggle them about to make an attractive arrangement, leaving room to label them clearly. Photographs can be cropped to take out any unnecessary bits such as too much sky and special photographs could be mounted on a background to enhance the colours. You might even decide to add stickers or other decorative effects to enhance the arrangement.

Producing your Life Book as part of a group can also be fun. Some companies encourage people to create memory books and even provide a consultant to help groups of people who want to work collectively on their Life Books. Why not get together with a friend and make working on your Life Book a joint venture?

To Sum Up

• A Life Book can contain anything interesting about your life and times that will lie flat.
• Concentrate on including things that have changed significantly over time.
• Enhance the collection by decorating the pages with stickers, drawings, or other decorations.

AN AUDIO RECORD

Imagine how exciting it would be to find a cassette, play it, and hear the voice of your grandfather who died more than 20 years ago. Perhaps you have only a hazy memory of him. It might be that he was talking about his life and the work he had done. Perhaps he had been a railway worker and had stories to tell about the railways. Or perhaps he had seen active service in the Second World War and had memories of that. Lots of people have written about both these subjects but this would be a very personal view - and from a member of your own family too.

Most people would agree that there is a genetic influence in the sound of people's voices. This is most obvious in recorded speech or on the phone. How often have you telephoned someone and mistaken the person who has answered for the person you want? It turns out that the person answering is either a parent, a son or daughter, or sibling. Voices can sound almost identical within families. How intriguing then, if, when you heard your ancestor's recorded voice, you had the added bonus of it sounding very similar to your own.

You will find that an audio recording can communicate something very special. The sound of the voice, the little interjections, the laughs, the incidental non-verbal sounds, even the pauses, all contribute to capturing a moment in time and the personal view of a life which, were it not for the recording, would be lost forever.

By spending just a small amount of time now you can make sure that descendants of yours have the pleasure of hearing your voice and learning, directly from you, about your life and times in years to come. Alternatively, you could make a recording of a relative talking about his or her life and times. Remember, though, that if you choose to record an older person, memories are likely to be more accurate if you do not leave it until they are too old and possibly a little confused.

You could undertake this task in just one evening, or even in as little as a couple of hours! So why not get going?

Getting Started

The starting point is to get hold of some reasonably high-quality recording equipment. If you have an audio system at home with a microphone and recording capability, you are ready. If not, a small portable cassette recorder can be bought cheaply. Portability of the equipment permits a wide choice of locations for the recording. If you are going to take the trouble to make a recording, it is worth making sure that the equipment you are using produces a good result; with this in mind you might decide that you need a separate microphone rather than the built-in microphone that portable cassette recorders usually have.

Make sure you find a quiet place where you will not be disturbed. You don't want someone to come in and talk to you, or even to shout from the other room, when you are in the middle of recording.

If you feel unsure about what you would like to talk about, look through the list of suggestions given later in this section to get some idea of the topics you would like to cover. If you are interviewing another family member you could take along some photographs to get them started.

Anyone who finds the idea of recording 'cold' difficult might like to be interviewed by somebody else. In that case the interviewer, beforehand, can go through the list of topics that the person wants to include. The interviewer will then be able to help the conversation along and prompt when necessary. This method can also be used for interviewing other family members and is particularly good for older people, whose memories might not be as good as they were and who might need a little help with recording.

145

Remember not to overwhelm the person you are interviewing. You don't need to cover everything in one recording session - you can always come back. Also, try to listen carefully and ask questions about anything that is unclear. You have probably seen good and bad interviews on the television. A good interviewer listens to the answer and is not too quick to press on to the next question. He is always ready to delve further into something that's interesting.

Practise

Practise recording something for about a minute or two - you might like to describe something you did recently. Play the recording back and decide whether your voice is at the right volume and whether you need to speak more quickly or slowly. People new to recording often speak too fast. Just make sure that what you are saying is audible. It would be a good idea to ask someone for his or her opinion on how you sound.

Content

Before you start you will need to give a little thought to what you are going to say. If you are comfortable with speaking and find that your words flow easily, you might decide to jot down just a few headings of what you would like to cover. Alternatively, you might want to write out a comprehensive 'script' before starting. Or perhaps something between the two would suit you best. Have a look at the ideas that follow and think about what you would like to include.

A Complete Résumé of Your Life So Far - An Audio Autobiography

If you do this, you will almost certainly want to make extensive notes. Remember to include only those things you feel reasonably confident your descendants will be interested in. The name of your best friend at school will only be of interest if it is coupled with stories of what you did and why you liked her. Give emphasis to anything that describes the times in which you are living - and be sure to include any aspects of the world that have changed dramatically during your lifetime. See Parts III and VI for more ideas on this.

Here are some topics you might like to include:

- Anything you know about your ancestors
- A description of the house/flat and area where you were born
- A description of your early family life
- Childhood games and pastimes
- Your education and a description of your school
- Teenage years
- Food you enjoy
- Clothes you wear
- Hobbies
- Favourite music/books
- Work - the jobs you do or have done
- Marriage
- Children
- What gives you pleasure
- What worries you
- Health - physical and mental well-being
- Something about your personality - what sort of person are you?

If you decide on this comprehensive format, it may well run to several cassettes so you will have to take a lot of care in packaging them to make sure they don't get separated over the years. You should also edit the recordings to eliminate any unwanted intrusions or uninteresting sections.

A Concise Autobiography

If time is limited you could make a shorter audio recorded autobiography, in which case you can concentrate on just a few topics that are of real interest to you. In this way you would be including just enough to keep a future family historian happy. (See 'An Alternative Autobiography' in Part III.)

Your Favourite Things

The idea here is to talk about some of the things that make life pleasurable for you. If any of the subjects in the list above particularly appeal to you, you could take one or two and expand on them. It might be listening to music, reading, painting, or some other hobby. Or it could be your job, or simply spending time at home with the family. Future generations will be sure to be interested in how families at the beginning of the 21st century spent their time. Presumably things will continue to change in family homes as they have done over the past 50 years with the coming of television and computers!

A Holiday or Favourite Place

If this appeals to you, you could consider actually making a recording while you are on holiday or at your favourite place. Not a bad way to spend an hour in your hotel room after a day of sightseeing in an especially beautiful city you have just discovered. Imagine how it would bring the whole thing to life if you found a recording of your grandfather which he had actually made while camping in a quiet valley in an unspoilt part of the country, or just as he returned from his first holiday abroad. It would be particularly interesting if it was an area you knew - although, of course, by now it might not be quite so unspoilt!

The appeal of the natural world is universal and timeless. Even if some sights have changed and become more commercialised this can still be true - the magnificence and wonder of the Niagara Falls or the Grand Canyon has no doubt moved generations of tourists in a very similar way. For this reason it will not be necessary to describe the place in detail but rather to say something about how you feel about it - the emotions it evokes in you.

Of course, like looking through someone else's holiday snaps, holiday stories can be boring. So, remember the golden rule of not meandering around in lots of boring detail, but keep your mind set on what it is about the place that future generations might find interesting. Always keep your future audience in mind.

Christmas or a Family Festival

This is where you can really have some fun! When all the family is gathered together you can take turns in recording and so send a whole family message down the centuries. Again, just imagine how good it would be to have a recording, perhaps made soon after you were born, with contributions from different family members and anyone else who happened to be there. It would be best to warn the contributors in advance so that they could be prepared - they might like to think about and make some notes on what they want to say.

A Special Occasion

Do you think that on the eve of your wedding you could take a little time to record something of what is going on around you? Wouldn't it have been wonderful if your great-grandmother had been able to do that? Perhaps something about the plans for the wedding and about hopes for the future, what she was wearing and who was attending the wedding.

If time is limited and you do not liking writing, an audio recording would be a very effective way of communicating something of your life and times. In a single evening you could record a lot of valuable information about yourself and your life onto an audio cassette which, if properly labelled and kept safe, would make a very interesting Gift.

Editing and Organising Your Audio Records

You will want your recordings to be accessible and well ordered for your listeners. Be sure to indicate what the content is so that the location of particular parts can be found. For an audio cassette, you can make a list of the various sections of the recording and write this on the cover. The means of creating CD audio recordings is now well within the reach of ordinary people at home, with the use of some editing software on a PC. CDs have the great facility of allowing you to easily locate particular tracks.

Transcripts

There are a number of advantages to transcribing the recording as a written account. You can edit some of the content, by excluding the breaks, pauses and interruptions; you can add explanatory notes, for example to identify someone who is mentioned by the speaker; and you can include some commentary about the occasion or circumstances of the interview. A great advantage of the written transcript is that it can easily be copied and distributed as a separate memento. It will be, in itself, a useful factual resource for those interested in the family's history.

To Sum Up

- If you are short of time an audio recording is easy and quick to make.
- For a good result invest in some good quality recording equipment.
- Find a quiet place to make the recording.
- Prepare a list of topics to be covered.
- Edit the recording.
- If there is more than one cassette, package them carefully together and label them clearly.
- Make a transcript of what has been said.

CAPTURING A MOMENT IN TIME

One Christmas afternoon, at a family gathering, a tape was played where the grandfather (Charlie), who had died several years previously, was talking about his life and times. The recording had been made very easily one evening when the old man was on a visit to his son, just a year before he died. He was talking very simply, in a relaxed way, about his life, his work and his family. He made some jokes, laughed a lot, and obviously enjoyed the experience of reminiscing. You can't believe how the faces of family members lit up when they heard his voice!

The following transcript of a part of that interview shows the special way in which such a recording can reflect the flavour of somebody's life and how they perceive the world.

Interviewer (Charlie's son): Tell me something about your early years - what work did you do?

Charlie: I had some greenhouses with my brother Bill.

Interviewer: How old were you then?

Charlie: Let's see - I was going out with Lizzie Bristow then. I was in my 20s. We grew about three tons of tomatoes. People came from miles around to the greenhouses to buy them. Nobody else was selling them then so we could sell as many as we could grow. When they get talking about greenhouses down the pub I tell them all about it. It was expensive though. We had to pay for the plants and the manure and then there were the water rates.

Interviewer: What went wrong? How long did you have the greenhouses?

Charlie: About two years - then we grew cress and wallflowers. I knew all about them. I used to read it all up. My brother Bill had a motor bike and side-car. He never used to ride it. He used to let me ride it. Once we got in the dyke (ditch) - those were the days (laughter). I had a Morgan runabout then.

Interviewer: What was a Morgan?

Charlie: A 3-wheel-car.

Interviewer: You drove it, but I don't think you ever got a car licence?

Charlie: No there were no car licences in them days. There weren't really any cars - we had motor bikes. No cars in my early days. I've seen some troubles in my time - there was that time I broke my femur.

Interviewer: Yes, you slid off the roof. How old were you then - about 60?

Charlie: No - it was before I was 60. They rushed me off to the hospital in King's Lynn and got me on the x-ray. I had to stay in the hospital for over a week. I've often thought I could write a book - write a book about my life - what I've been through. I left school when I was 13. My mother used to do the washing then, my mother did, for the Osborns.

Interviewer: Who were the Osborns then?

Charlie: They're still there. They've got the furniture shop in town. I started working for them as a French polisher but I got the polisher's colic. I had to pack that in.

Interviewer: That was straight from school was it?

Charlie: Yes, you had to get a certificate to leave school. I went to Ramnoth Road School. Before that I'd gone to a school that had been opened by Johnny Young's wife at the Church. Father Page was very happy about that. I never got the chance to go in for much when I left school. I used to say to Molly (Charlie's wife) - 'Where did the brains come from?' She was a brainy woman. She was a fighter. She saw in the paper that the old age pensioners in the town needed some help and she went to see the editor and got all the pensioners together. It started with just three old men. Then she went to the Metal Box and she started the Unions there. When we lived in Emneth your Mum used to walk from Emneth to Wisbech where she worked at Smedley's. Seven mile round trip. If you told them that today...

Interviewer: To get back to the greenhouses, what happened?

Charlie: Well, we put a lot of money aside and some old bloke stole it. He was a drunken bugger and he stole the money. That was the end of that. We couldn't raise any more money. Then Bill got married. He got married at the Registry Office, then he went to the Catholic Church.

Interviewer: What did you do after you left the French polishing?

Charlie: That's when I started in the building trade. I went to Elworthy's. There were a lot of people working there. That's the time when we started going singing round the pubs. I've always really enjoyed singing - I've sung for nearly 50 years in the church choir. When we went to the pubs we was known as the 'Threesome'. There was old Doug Price on the piano and Bill Pryor used to play his little old banjo. Those were good times.

Did you see your Mum's picture when she put up for the Council? It rained hard all that day. She didn't want to go on the Council but they talked her into it. A wonderful woman she was.

Interviewer: When did she first get interested in the Labour Party?

Charlie: Oh, she'd always been interested - she used to go to their meetings in the Park. But I don't understand now why everyone votes Tory. They're working class yet they vote Tory. Can't understand it. That old Maggie Thatcher, she got in under false pretences. Just wanted to be the first woman Prime Minister. I met her - in King's Lynn. I always remember, when we lived at Emneth, Molly went to speak at a meeting and these Liberal people came over to heckle her. She dealt with them - she was a wonderful woman. I always remember that.

Interviewer: What were your best years? Were they before the War?

Charlie: Yes, that spoilt everything. I always remember Bob Ringer and Cal Lodden going to join up. I was going with them. That was in '39. But instead of that there was a sewer that was bunged up in Verdun Road so I had to go and do that, so that's why I never went to the war. Bob said, 'We'll be getting a holiday,' but instead of that he got in the hands of the Japs. I wanted to join up but they said I was in a reserved occupation. They said I was doing more good than I would have in the Army.

Interviewer: Did everyone think it was going to be over and done with quickly?

Charlie: Yes. And what would a war be like today if it came along? Churchill was the Prime Minister then. And then there was Nye Bevan, Aneurin Bevan, one of the greatest men who ever lived. I saw a programme about him on the telly the other day - a great man. Did you ever go in Westminster Cathedral?

Interviewer: Yes, I remember going up to London with you. That must have been about 1950. We went to Westminster Cathedral then. I remember us taking some photographs there. They didn't come out very well. The trolley buses were going then. But we don't have them now.

Charlie: No, we don't have the trams either.

Interviewer: Then we went to see somebody at Bromley.

Charlie: That was Uncle Nelson. Then we visited relatives in Catford and Leigh Green. I don't remember their names, but one of them died the next year - he was electrocuted working on the Underground...

Although this transcript is a little short on factual information - much of which had been lost in the memory of this 80-year-old - the essence of the occasion, with a middle-aged son interviewing his elderly father, is captured sensitively and says a lot.

PART V

RESEARCHING YOUR FAMILY HISTORY

RESEARCHING YOUR ANCESTRY

Although you are concentrating here on your own life and times, it is important to remember that, to some extent, your past has made you what you are. You are the repository of much valuable family information and you might be in a position to gather lots more information now about your family from older relatives who are still alive. They may have information about your ancestry going back to the early years of the 20th century.

First of all, a word about the difference between 'genealogy' and 'family history'. A genealogist is an investigator who searches for clues about ancestry. He is dedicated to tracing a family back through the generations, his ultimate aim being to produce a family tree going back as far as possible. A family historian, on the other hand, is the one who puts the flesh on the bones of a genealogy. He is interested in the stories that surround individual members of a family. A family historian aims to gather together the story of the family and the family traditions to pass on to future generations.

You will need to think about how far back you want to go in tracing your family roots. Even going back five generations, about 120 years, to your great-great-grandparents will give you some idea of how quickly one person can grow into quite a crowd! You can see that if you make the decision to research your family history, something that started out as an innocent enquiry can very soon turn into a serious time-consuming hobby.

There has been great interest in recent years in genealogy and family history and there are many books, websites and computer software packages available. Family historians have been at work in far corners of the world, so whether your family is locally based or has roamed the globe, you can get help in your search for information simply by turning to the Internet or by referring to the Reading List in Appendix 1. If you have a computer there are software packages to help you with the task. There are also magazines dedicated to genealogy and family history which are full of useful information, tips and advertisements.

There are three general approaches to a genealogical search and to preserving information about your family history for future generations.

Simply Include What You Know Yourself

Think again about what information you would like to have received from your own grandparents and consider this: if your grandmother had written down, say when she was 30, all she knew about her parents (your great-grandparents) and her grandparents (your great-great-grandparents), wouldn't that information have been interesting to you now? She might even have known something about her great-grandparents (your great-great-great-grandparents). If only she had written a few paragraphs on a single piece of paper, and kept it safely, she would have saved future family historians a great deal of work.

So, you could produce an invaluable Gift for your descendants simply by spending an hour now writing down all you know about your immediate and more distant family members, including cousins and second cousins. If the only things you know about an individual are their name and where they lived that would be enough. It is important to say whether the information is recorded simply from memory (in which case there might be inaccuracies) or whether it has been verified by documentation - perhaps birth or death certificates.

There are several different ways of recording the information and these will be discussed later. By taking just a little time now you could produce something that future generations will no doubt consider as pure treasure. And what a lot of trouble it would save them if they wanted to trace their ancestry.

Interviews with Your Parents/Grandparents

You could get still more information if you are prepared to spend a little more time. Depending on your age you may be in contact with your parents and grandparents. They are a very helpful source of family information, so you can get started by interviewing this valuable 'primary source'.

The *Information Sheets* included in this book are divided into two: those covering information of a factual nature and those dealing with thoughts and feelings. You could ask older family members to complete a *Factual Information Sheet*, which gives quite a lot of life details. They might not want to complete all the sections so you could make an amended version that is shorter and includes simply their names, dates and places of birth, latest address and something about their occupation. The important point is to get some information about everyone. The individual sheets can be stored with the family tree when you get round to producing it.

If you want to include more than pure facts, the *Thoughts & Feelings Information Sheets* could also be completed by a family member. Some relatives, however, may find this exercise a little uncomfortable. People often find it easy to answer questions of a factual nature, but when it comes to questions about their relationships, thoughts, feelings and so on, they might be a little reluctant to open up. Trying to extract such information from people can be difficult and is potentially sensitive territory, so you may have to concentrate simply on factual information. While talking to your parents or grandparents you could uncover some 'skeletons in the cupboard' and you will, of course, need to be sensitive as to how far to probe. The section on 'Emotional Impact' aims to help here (see Part I).

If, on the other hand, you are very close to the people you interview, they might be prepared to say something about how they see themselves, their strengths and weaknesses, how they relate to others, what causes them anxiety, and how they deal with problems. If this is the case then you may think about asking them to complete some sections of the *Thoughts & Feelings Information Sheets*. After all, this is the very stuff that will bring an individual to life for future generations, but do tread gently.

An alternative to completing the *Information Sheets* with older relatives would be to find out about their lives by chatting to them and making notes which you later type up. And/or you could use a tape recorder or even a video camera.

During your interviews with family members you should ask to see any registration certificates - birth, marriage or death - that they have in their possession. It is always important when recording information for the benefit of future generations to say whether it is simply hearsay or whether it has been validated by certification which you have inspected. Also, remember to ask them whether they know of any more distant relative who has done work on your family tree - you don't want to carry out the work unnecessarily if research has already been done.

Once you have completed your interviews you could make a very useful Gift by producing a family tree (see guidelines later) and keeping it with the completed *Information Sheets* and any recordings you have made.

Further Research

If, by now, you have become interested in the task of recording your family history, you might decide that you would like to take things further and expand on the information jointly held by you and your immediate family. There are a number of possible sources of information.

National Civil Registration

The amount of information available, and the sophistication of the systems used to collate and store that information, varies considerably and will depend on where you live and where your ancestors lived. Many countries have in place a compulsory civil registration system dating back to the middle or latter part of the 19th century. These records are normally available for the interested individual to visit and inspect. Copies of certificates are also normally available - often by post.

Man has always been nomadic and an understanding of population movement will be illuminating for anyone searching for his family's roots. During the past three centuries, the availability of transport made it possible for millions of people to leave their homelands in search of a better life overseas. In the first half of the 19th century most of the new settlers in the USA were from England, whereas during the second half of the century most were Irish or German. Movement was generally due to difficult circumstances in the immigrants' homelands. Europeans also settled in Canada, Australia, Africa and New Zealand. Millions of Irish people left home from the time of the potato famines onwards, many of them settling in mainland Britain. The Scots, Welsh and English travelled across the globe to seek their fortune. Many millions left mainland Europe, often to settle in countries that fellow countrymen had colonised. Thus the French often headed for Canada and the Spanish for South America.

Another important factor adding to the complexity of tracing ancestry is that national boundaries have been, and still are, constantly changing. Many present-day European nation states were, prior to 1918, part of the Austro-Hungarian Empire. In 1922, Ireland was divided into two meaning that archive records were segregated. A branch of your family, at one time traceable through the archives of one country, will seem to disappear if the part of the country in which they were living became annexed by a neighbour.

Crucial also for the family historian is an understanding of how and where demographic information is stored.

It was not until 1837 that civil registration began in England and Wales, and even then it was not a complete record because registration was not compulsory. From 1874 onwards there was a legal requirement to register births, marriages and deaths, so records became much more comprehensive and are a more reliable source for the family historian.

Scotland's civil registration began in 1858, with the records for the whole of Scotland being kept at New Registry House in Edinburgh. Births and deaths began being registered in Northern Ireland in 1864, but the records for marriages only go back to 1922.

In the USA, tracing the registration of births, marriages and deaths is complicated by the fact that the country is largely populated by immigrants who arrived over a long period of time, from diverse backgrounds and widely varying geographical regions. Registration is the responsibility of each state and a good starting place would be the state archives located in the state capital. Although the period when registration began varies from state to state, certificates are usually available from the early years of the 20th century. County court-houses can help with registrations before that time.

There are a variety of arrangements for the inspection of registration certificates, so you could save time by making a phone call for information and advice before you visit. Charges vary and you might well be able to obtain a copy of a certificate by post.

Using the Census Records

From pre-biblical times the State or the Crown has been interested in counting populations and recording where they live, their occupations and their places of birth. Modern-day governments have chosen to collect more information to help them in planning services such as schools and housing. Such information is available in most countries throughout the world and is invaluable to the family historian.

The first census to be of any use to the family historian in England and Wales took place in 1841 and this has been followed by a census every ten years, except in 1941, as this was during the Second World War. The Registrar General in Scotland holds very similar census returns, although the picture for Ireland is less complete. Much of the Irish census documentation was destroyed during military action in Dublin at the beginning of the 20th century.

From as early as 1790, the USA collected the names of the head of each household, in order to determine representation in the House of Representatives. From 1850 onwards, every person in the household was included, together with information about their age, sex, race, occupation and place of birth. One way for the family researcher to access this information is through the National Archive Microfilm Rental Program, although many libraries hold the records for their own state.

Census data that is available in Europe varies from country to country. In France, some information prior to the French Revolution is available, but a regular census did not begin until 1836. From that year onwards, a census has been taken every five years, except for 1916 and 1941 because of the wars.

In Germany since the 16th century the census has taken the form of 'Town Rolls' which list all the citizens in the larger towns. Tracing ancestors here is helped by the fact that for centuries, ordinary people were not allowed to move from one area to another without permission.

Apart from those who emigrated to the United States, Italians in centuries gone by tended to stay put so they do not have too much trouble tracing their family history. Local registration documents and graveyards will provide lots of information about their ancestry.

A good way to trace a foreign ancestor is to start with the census data for the mother country.

Religious Records

In the United Kingdom, some Church of England parish registers go back as far as 1538 (1552 for Scotland) when Thomas Cromwell issued an injunction that records of baptisms, marriages and burials should be kept by the clergy. Similarly, in France, the oldest parish registers date back to the first half of the 16th century when they were kept by the parish priest. If you are able to inspect copies of certificates issued to mark these 'rites of passage', you will glean much valuable information. From baptism certificates, you also will learn the parents' Christian names and surnames, their place of abode and their trade or profession.

If you are not able to trace your ancestors through parish registers, it might be that they are of a different belief - Jewish, Islamic, Mormon - or, indeed, of no belief whatsoever. In the United Kingdom many Non Conformist registers of baptisms, marriages and burials prior to 1837 were passed to the Public Record Office in London, so these might be worth examining.

Church of Jesus Christ of Latter-Day Saints' Family History Centres

Because the Mormons, as members of the Church of Jesus Christ of Latter-Day Saints are commonly called, have an obligation to trace their ancestors in order to baptise them and give them salvation by proxy, the Church has established Family History Centres which have proved to be a valuable resource for family historians throughout the world. From small beginnings in the

USA in 1938 they now have nearly 3,000 libraries containing genealogical information in more than 50 countries.

To build up the International Genealogical Index, known as the IGI, Mormons have travelled all over the world to copy parish registry entries. The index currently contains entries for more than 240 million people worldwide. Most of the information covers the periods from 1550-1920 so it does not include many living people.

If you were really keen you could visit the vast collection of records held by the Mormons in huge humidity and temperature-controlled underground caverns at Utah in the USA, but a simpler way to get access would be from CD-Roms that you can buy, or via the Internet (see below).

Other sources of information

Having exhausted all of these sources of information you still have other avenues to explore - wills, records of educational establishments, professional records, workhouse, hospital and asylum records, criminal records, Press reports, land and property registers, the armed forces records, coats of arms. Enough to make genealogy a lifetime's pursuit!

If you are keen to expand your knowledge of your family history still further you could join one of the Family History Societies that exist in a number of countries. In the United States there are hundreds of genealogy societies made up of people from all nationalities and creeds. The Society of Genealogists in the UK holds information about three million people and has the largest

169

collection of genealogical books and material in the country.

Tracing Your Family 'Online'

If tracing your family tree sounds like hard work, don't despair - if you have access to a computer then help is at hand. If not, you might try to encourage another family member who does use a computer to become involved in the project with you. The computer will not do your research for you but it will certainly make life easier by helping you to get the information and store it.

It has been said that by using a computer you can now complete in a couple of weeks research that would have previously taken a year. Websites and CD-Roms make genealogical information more readily accessible as well as helping with the practical task of presenting the information in the form of a family tree. With all this help at hand, it is relatively simple for most people to trace their family back to at least the mid-19th century.

There is such a wealth of information available on the Internet that, for the beginner, the question is often - 'Where should I start?'

There are literally hundreds of websites to explore, but a lot of the hard work has been done for you and is neatly catalogued on just one or two sites. A vast amount of addresses and information can be obtained from: Cyndi's List on www.CyndisList.com and Genuki on www.genuki.org.uk.

Computer packages are also available that give you access to a massive amount of genealogical information. See also Appendix 2 for a list of useful addresses and website details.

To Sum Up

- The story of your life starts with your ancestors.
- You will help future family historians by recording now what you know about your family, past and present.
- If you are prepared to spend a little more time, ask other family members to add what they know.
- Always state whether the information is from memory or whether there are certificates from which you can verify the data.
- Search other genealogical data banks such as public records and the IGI.
- Massive genealogical data banks are available on the Internet and on computer packages.

MAKING A FAMILY TREE

As you start collecting information about past family members, you will have to think about how to present it. Everybody is familiar with the idea of a 'family tree' and you will get a sense of satisfaction as soon as you start to set down on paper the structure of your own family. A family tree can be designed by hand, but you might prefer to use a computer software package. There are a number on the market that provide ready-to-use family tree charts which allow you to drop in your own family details and print them out. If you do not use a computer yourself you might enlist the help of a friend or family member.

Producing a family tree can either take a little work (a couple of hours and a few phone calls) or a great deal of time and effort.

The Minimal Approach

This would be to compile a family tree as far as you know it. By simply recording the names, dates and places of birth of yourself, your spouse, your siblings, your parents, and possibly your grandparents, you will save a potential family researcher a lot of hard work in years to come. This information can so quickly be lost. For example, it's amazing just how many people do not know the maiden name of their grandmother, even if the question is asked just a few years after her death.

Again, it is important that you make a note of whether the information you are inputting is from your memory or whether you have inspected certificates that verify the dates. Any serious future family historian will need to know which is the case.

Try to consider compiling a simple family tree based on what you know as a very worthwhile task rather than a 'second best' effort. You may intend to 'do it properly' when you have the time, but might never get around to it and, after all, some information is better than none.

The following examples show just how easy it can be to create a simple family tree.

Examples of a Basic Family Tree

This family tree might typify what you could produce from recall without more research. It covers just four generations and some of the information is incomplete.

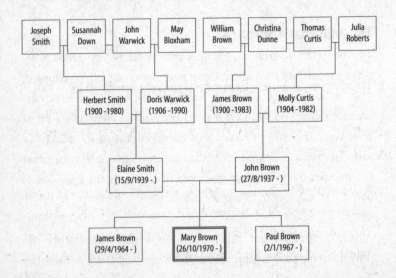

The same information could be presented using circles and semi-circles, although this type of family tree can only include the parents of each descendant - there is no room for brothers and sisters.

Producing a More Comprehensive Family Tree

This will take time and you will need to do a bit of work, but you can get help with this task from one of the many computer software applications available.

Some of these applications are free but those with the most useful features might have to be purchased. However, dabbling with *any* software package for creating a family tree would get you started. When you have been inputting your family data for a while you will discover how a particular application performs and what sort of output can be obtained. It might well be that you are disappointed with your first results but the exercise will be worthwhile since it will have given you a 'wish list' of features to be included in your ideal family tree software. Then, by reading reviews, discussing preferences of other family historians and examining specifications, you will be in a more confident position to buy a package that suits your needs.

Family tree applications always take, as their basic input, records for each individual with details such as birth date, birth place, date of marriage, marriage partner etc. Other inputs can include images and even sounds, but perhaps the final result can only be fully appreciated if you see it for yourself on a computer.

To Sum Up

• You could create a family tree either by hand or by using a computer software application.

• If you don't have time to create a comprehensive family tree, at least make a note of what you *do* know and save valuable information from being lost.

• Try out some of the free family tree packages and then ask around about other people's preferences before purchasing one to suit your needs.

• Textual family tree information can be supplemented by images and sounds.

PART VI

THIS ALL HAPPENED IN MY LIFETIME

CHANGES DURING A LIFETIME

You probably have little idea what was happening in the world when your great-grandmother was young. Perhaps she lived in a country where extreme political change led to her having to move, perhaps becoming a refugee. Perhaps she had to sit separated from white people because she lived at a time when segregation rules did not allow for the mixing of whites and blacks. Perhaps she got very excited when gas was brought into her home to illuminate the dark evenings. Perhaps her life was plagued by a painful medical condition for which there was then no help. Perhaps several of her children died in early infancy because of some disease which has since been eradicated. It would be interesting to know something of how the changes that occurred while she was alive affected her day-to-day life and what her preoccupations were. If this is something that would interest you, then why not do a little work now to ensure that your own descendants have some idea of the changes that were occurring during your lifetime?

Now, at the beginning of the 21st century, the pace of change has increased to such a degree that many people have difficulty in keeping up with modern technological advances and the social changes that often come in their wake.

Changes that have occurred during your lifetime will have been more or less extreme depending on where you live but, nonetheless, they are the dramatic backcloth against which you have lived your life. In some cases 'progress' has had a devastating effect on the lives of people and their environment. For example, in some parts of the world huge dams have been built to create reservoirs, leaving whole towns under water and making thousands of people homeless. Imagine telling your great-grandchildren that for hundreds of years generations of your family had lived in a village which is now at the bottom of a reservoir! Or perhaps your family's village has now been flattened to make way for a housing development - where they once tended goats and grew fruit there are now several hundred houses!

To get some grasp of just how much the world has changed during the lifetime of someone who is 60 or over, bear in mind that they were born before: t-shirts, ballpoint pens, computers, microwave ovens, the State of Israel, colour television, man's exploration of space, car seat belts, the polio vaccine, the atomic bomb, the electric guitar, lasers (leading to bar codes), the heart/lung machine, video recorders and video games, and lots more! There are plenty of websites giving timelines devoted to specialist areas. You might find a visit to www.history 1900s.about.com very fruitful.

It is difficult to imagine where technological change will lead and what life will be like in another 100 years. Whether you are 20 or 60, the world in which you are living now has almost certainly changed considerably since you were a child. You can safely speculate that your grandchildren will live out their lives in a world far removed from that in which you are living today.

Life for most people in the past was far more predictable than it is today. For centuries before the Industrial Revolution people were generally born in the same place that their parents and grandparents had been born. In some countries it was even against the law for ordinary people to move to a different locality. Local churchyards, especially those in country areas, are full of generation after generation of the same family. Family members often followed the same occupations. Life now is much more unpredictable. People move around far more, not only within their own country but from continent to continent. Change is endemic in modern society.

The nature of change in society as the world moves into the 21st century is very much dictated by global capitalism. This means that whether you live in the cold open spaces of northern Europe, a small town in the United States, or the sophisticated centre of Rome, the forces of change will, in many ways, have a remarkably similar impact on your life. An evening at home with fast food and a video, contacting friends across the world via email, mobile phones, taking the children to school in a 4 x 4 are all part of the daily round.

An interesting talking point is to ask people what change has been the most significant for them during the course of their lifetime. One respondent said, 'Replacement hips and hearing aids,' and that was because her husband had been the recipient of both and his life would have been far less pleasant if it had not been for these advances in medical technology. Another said that the most significant change for her had been the demise of local industry. The closure of a large manufacturing company had more or less been the death of the small town in which she and generations of her family before her had lived, and she had had to move away in search of work. A third, who had been brought up in a quiet little town in the South of France, recounted how tourism had changed the face of everything that was familiar to her as a girl.

What changes that have been significant during the course of *your* lifetime do you think your descendants might be interested in? There are three possible approaches to describing these changes:

1. You could describe how particular changes have affected your life - a personal view.

2. You could do some research and give the facts about changes that have occurred during your lifetime - a factual account.

3. You could include both of these - a personal account backed up by the facts.

A collection of writings about particular changes in your lifetime would make an interesting section in your 'alternative' autobiography as suggested in Part III.

To Sum Up

• The world in which your descendants will grow up will certainly be very different from the world you are experiencing today.

• A record of the changes occurring in the world during your lifetime will be of interest to your descendants.

• Your personal reflections on change will bring social history alive.

CHANGES IN THE 20TH CENTURY

Because people's day-to-day lives are very much tied up within the society and times in which they live, your Gift will be all the more interesting if you reflect on and describe something of the social changes that you and your family have witnessed and are witnessing. Such writings would make an interesting addition to your 'alternative' autobiography. The following topics are designed to help you think about what changes have been significant during your lifetime.

Health Care

The 20th century saw huge advances in medical knowledge and techniques. What advances have significantly affected you and your way of life? Perhaps you are alive today as a result of advances in medical technology. Perhaps you had a difficult birth and would, in bygone days, have died soon afterwards.

It was only at the beginning of the 20th century that different types of blood were identified and there began to be an understanding that diseases could be caused by the lack of certain substances in the diet. The discovery of penicillin in 1928 meant that many diseases that previously killed could be treated. This was followed by the development of vaccines against a whole range of previously fatal diseases. Huge numbers of the population were vaccinated against such diseases as polio, diphtheria, tetanus, measles, mumps, rubella and influenza. The 20th century saw polio vanquished, smallpox eradicated and the incidence of cholera and tuberculosis severely reduced. What vaccinations did you and your children have?

Life expectancy has risen faster this century than ever before - in England and Wales it rose from 66.4 years (for men) and 71.5 years (for women) in 1950, to 74.1 and 79.4 respectively in 1995. When your great-grandparents were having babies, say at the beginning of the 20th century, there was every likelihood that several of their children would die very soon after birth. Today, thanks to improved public health and nutrition and enormous advances in medicine, this is very uncommon in the developed countries of the world.

Prior to the 1950s heart surgery was very limited, but by 1953 the first heart/lung machine made it possible to conduct surgery while by-passing the patient's own heart and lungs. This was followed in 1967 by the first heart transplant operation, while in 1972 the first kidney donor schemes were introduced. Have you or any family member benefited from these improvements in medical practice?

Customs and arrangements for childbirth in developed countries have changed dramatically in terms of how and where women have their babies. These changes can be seen in the increasing 'medicalisation' of childbirth - that is, the whole process is a medical procedure with medical professionals being prominent players. Years ago women had babies 'naturally' at home, but it is now much more likely that children will be delivered in hospital and that the whole process will be very much under the supervision of medical staff. Your descendants may well be interested to hear about your experiences of childbirth - where you had the baby and what, if any, medically intrusive procedures were involved.

While for most women prior to the second half of the 20th century the problem had been how to prevent too many pregnancies, there were always those couples who desperately wanted a child but could not conceive. Help came for them in 1977 when in-vitro fertilisation was first performed. By 1978 came the first 'test tube baby'.

Your descendants will be interested to know if you have had first-hand experience of the improvements in health care.

Agriculture

The lives of people in areas that are predominantly agricultural have changed beyond recognition during the last 100 years. If you were born into an agricultural community in North America or Europe, many of the agricultural jobs will have disappeared and your family may have moved in search of work; the local shops and school may well have closed and small farms and large estates have most likely given way to huge holdings managed by large companies. Farms that used to be seen as rural idylls have been replaced by farms more reminiscent of industrial complexes, with their intensive-farming methods for both crops and animals.

Many changes have been made possible by the introduction of tractors. For centuries horses were used as energy on farms and it was only between the two World Wars that horses gave way to tractors on farms in the USA and Australia. In most parts of Europe it was even later. With mechanisation came previously unimaginable change:

- The amount of land under cultivation has increased dramatically.
- Hedges and trees have been pulled out to make way for ever larger fields.
- Drains have been laid under wetlands which were previously unsuitable for cultivation.
- All kinds of machines are used to apply fertilisers and pesticides and to harvest crops.

If you grew up in an agricultural community and have experienced any such changes, your descendants will be interested to hear about it.

The 'Cold War'

Another period that a politically aware observer might like to comment on is the so-called 'Cold War'. The 'war' between Communism and Capitalism was played out in different arenas across the world, notably in Korea and Vietnam, Berlin and Cuba.

Perhaps you or a family member fought in Vietnam or Korea? What did it mean to you? Was it a war worth fighting? Who knows, war might be eliminated in the future and your descendants would be intrigued to read of your wartime experiences.

Environmental Degradation

Anyone born in the second half of the 20th century has seen the environment come to the top of the list of concerns that are preoccupying politicians, as well as many ordinary people across the globe.

How can you begin to think about the environmental degradation that has occurred during your lifetime? Newspapers worldwide tell stories of:

- Disasters that have damaged the environment on a huge scale often with loss of human life. These include massive oil spills from tankers causing catastrophic damage to marine life.
- People demonstrating, and sometimes taking direct action, against what they see as environmentally harmful schemes.
- Prophesies of Armageddon with the world being destroyed by a massive natural disaster (such as global warming and the melting of the ice caps) which has been brought about by man's actions.

Depending on where you live, you might have witnessed a decline in your environment, such as huge tracts of land being built on, either for homes, industrial uses or new roads. Huge areas of land might have become flooded when valleys were dammed to provide a reservoir. Quarries might now scar the landscape where once there were undulating fields. Areas of woodland or forest might have been cut down to make way for buildings or roads. The possibilities are endless. The point is - have you seen an improvement or a tragic decline in your local environment?

If we assume that future generations will find a better way to protect the environment, then our descendants might be astounded at our accounts of the damage we were prepared to inflict on the environment as the 20th century ended and we moved into the 21st. You might like to comment on such things as:

- The hole in the ozone layer and warnings about climate change.
- Destruction of the tropical rain forests.
- Nuclear accidents which have released radioactive material into the environment.
- Accidents with other toxic materials such as at Bhopal in India.
- The activities of Greenpeace as a leading protest movement.

Are you concerned about damage to the environment? Have you been involved in protesting about a scheme that you believe will be harmful to the environment? How do you think the world can deal with the predicted environmental disasters? Your descendants would be interested to hear your comments because you are living in the thick of it!

Mass Consumption and Waste Disposal

Closely allied to environmental degradation are the issues of material consumption and waste disposal. The second half of the 20th century saw a huge growth in packaging of all kinds and of the throw-away society. Whereas previously it had been common practice to get an appliance - whether it be a washing machine or a television - repaired, new production practices led to it becoming cheaper to actually purchase a new one. The 'throw-away' age had arrived.

What happened then to all the rubbish? As the 20th century drew to a close there were heated debates about how to dispose of waste. Landfill sites were no longer a viable option in many areas where land was in short supply. An alternative means of disposing of waste was to install incinerators to burn it, but there was considerable controversy about safety. It was suggested that the residue left after incineration was toxic as were the fumes given up into the atmosphere. There were appeals to:

- Reduce - use less packaging and buy less consumables.
- Re-use - pass an item on to someone else or use it again yourself.
- Re-cycle - dispose of waste in such a way that it could be recycled.

During the last few decades of the 20th century, schemes were introduced throughout the high-consumption countries to encourage people to take their waste to special re-cycling depots. Paper, glass, cardboard, plastics and textiles went into special containers to be taken off to plants and converted into new products.

What do you think about the 'throw-away' society? How do you dispose of your rubbish? Your descendants would be interested to know.

Food

Eating has to be a regular activity for all humans and will continue to be so for future generations - unless, of course, they choose to eliminate meals and get all their nutrition from tablets!

Central to any discussion of food at the start of the 21st century is the fact that the past 50 years have seen a dramatic contrast between populations in developed countries being overfed and suffering from obesity, and underdeveloped countries in other parts of the world where people are dying from starvation. Even in the developed world, however, there are concerns about the quality of the food being consumed and the fact that many food sources, notably the fish in the sea, are fast disappearing.

As the 20th century drew to a close the variety of foods in supermarkets and the way in which they were packaged far, far exceeded anything that could have been envisaged by your grandparents. Processed foods and ready-meals have changed the way we live. Some children are growing up without ever having eaten a home-cooked meal and a mother's daily cooking duties of 50 years ago are a thing of the past. John Humphry's *The Great Food Gamble* charts the changes in eating habits and farming techniques and looks at the high price he sees society paying for this increase in choice and convenience.

Have your eating habits changed since you were a child? What foods do you eat now that were not available before? Do you continue to make any of your mother's recipes?

Europe

Following the conflict in Europe during the Second World War, countries within the continent moved towards co-operation and unification. There was, however, considerable resistance in Britain to joining the European Economic Community when it was formed in 1957: Britain only joined in 1972. The British people were always cautious about what they saw as giving up their sovereignty to a European state. As the 20th century came to an end there was still considerable internal wrangling in both major political parties in the UK, who were split over whether they wanted Britain to apply for full membership of the European Monetary System.

If you are politically aware you might like to give your views on the debate about Europe at the start of the 21st century.

The 'Irish Problem'

Throughout the 20th century Ireland has rarely been out of the headlines. Those living in Northern Ireland have had their lives dominated by 'The Troubles'. For those living on the mainland, something that had been a distant problem came very close to home when the IRA bombing campaign began. The Irish question has challenged politicians in the UK for much of the 20th century. IRA bombings in Northern Ireland and on the mainland have claimed the lives of hundreds of civilians as politicians have struggled to find a solution. 1974 was a particularly bad year, with bombings in widespread locations, including many in Central London, Birmingham, Manchester and Guildford. The IRA assassinated Lord Mountbatten in 1979, and in 1984 an IRA bomb killed four people at the Conservative Party Conference. Then in 1998 there was the hope for peace when the Belfast agreement led to a power-sharing Executive at Stormont.

What are your views on the Irish problem? Have you been personally involved in some way - perhaps in the political debate or as an innocent victim? If so, write about it NOW.

Education

The school leaving age in the developed world has been steadily rising during the 20th century. In the UK it was raised from 14 in 1922, to 15 in 1947 and to 16 in 1972. Fashions in education are also constantly changing. Young children are sometimes taught by 'rote' with the children sitting in rows looking at the teacher. An alternative method is that of 'discovery' with the children sitting in small groups working independently. In the UK there has been a gradual increase in the number of people staying on in full-time education post 16 - the 1996/97 statistics show a figure of 75.4%. The number of males in full-time higher education in Great Britain doubled between 1970/71 and 1997/98, while the number of females in full-time higher education rose in the same period from 182,000 to 585,000.

If you are a grandparent you might like to write about your own experience of education compared with that of your grandchildren. Your great-grandchildren will then be able to compare their experiences with yours.

Changing Patterns of Employment

The second half of the 20th century was a time of considerable change in the economic structure of countries throughout the world. The major change in the economy of the USA, the UK and many other so-called 'developed' countries at this time was a dramatic decline in the manufacturing industry. The manufacturing base, with local communities working in the same industry for several generations, largely moved to the developing Asian countries where labour was cheaper. In the UK the number of employees in manufacturing fell by 43% between 1966 and 1991. This was accompanied by a rapid rise in service industries. In 1966 just under half of all employment in the UK was in services, whereas by 1991 this had risen to two-thirds. Peaks of unemployment were felt in 1931, 1980-85 and again in 1992.

Have you had a less than stable employment career? Have you suffered unemployment? Have you had to change your line of work? What help was available to you when you were unemployed?

Improvements in Housing

In every country in the developed world there has been modernisation of housing which has meant the installation of basic amenities where there were previously none. In the UK in 1947, 4.8 million houses had no fixed bath or shower, but by 1996 the figure had dropped to just 100,000. By the end of the 20th century 84% of homes had central heating.

Would you like to include a section comparing the accommodation you now enjoy with what you had during your

193

childhood? Did you have a tin bath in front of the fire? Did you have to go outside into the garden or yard to use the toilet?

Leisure

If we take leisure to mean the free time that is left after all paid and unpaid work has been done, we see an increase in leisure time during the period 1960-1990. In the UK, holiday entitlements for full-time manual workers rose substantially during that period. In 1960, 97% had just 2 weeks paid leave a year but by 1990, 64% received as much as 4-5 weeks. The number of people employed in the leisure industry is also an indicator of the growth in leisure pursuits. In 1950, just 212,000 worked in leisure, while by 1997 that figure had risen to 515,000.

Why not look at your pattern of holiday and weekend activities now compared with that of your family when you were a child? Your descendants will find it interesting to compare this with the way they are enjoying their leisure time, perhaps in the year 2020.

PERSONAL ACCOUNTS OF CHANGE

The following accounts each give a tantalising personal glimpse of how dramatic political and social changes have impacted on life during the late 20th century. If they were expanded and more detail was added, they would each make a very interesting 'Gift for the Future' for the descendants of the women who wrote them.

South Africa

A personal view of change by Louise Geddes, now living in Bishops Stortford in England

In the early years of my life I lived in a small town in South Africa called Ermelo, in the area then known as Transvaal. During the time that I grew up, the 1960s and early 1970s, I was aware of everyone being like myself. We all lived in very large homes with enormous gardens. Our employees, the gardener, the washing lady and child-minder, who were black, were part of the household. Our employees never lived on our premises, but on the 'location', which was within walking distance from our town - about a mile away. Everyone who lived or worked with us was always treated with respect, and I learnt from very early on to follow my parents' example. If workers wanted time off for private matters, this was honoured. They were paid respectable wages for those times and I always had to say 'please' and 'thank you', as I would to any other person. I learned how to iron from Christina who worked for our family for over 18 years. I also remember spending hours mastering this task by trying to iron my father's handkerchief. I recall digging alongside Mishak, our gardener, and helping him to plant and weed. At least, I thought I was helping him!

Although I grew up in a country that functioned differently, I myself had the rare privilege of having my home life and schooling include respect for all people regardless of race, culture and creed. In the late 1970s, however, I had no option but to relocate to the city of Johannesburg, as the convent school I attended had to close down. This was due to the then government who had banned any persons who advocated inclusion of racial cultures within education, or who advocated equality within religion, from entering South Africa. This policy, known as apartheid, prevented the school from recruiting any new teachers. Hence it was eventually forced to close for political and financial reasons.

In 1990 I left South Africa to live in England, a choice made for many personal reasons. Whenever I return 'home' I notice many changes on various levels. One major change is that the area I lived in is now known as Mapumalanga, and not the Transvaal. It is lovely to return home and be able to go and eat out with my child-minder who supported me with my son when I lived in South Africa. I could never have done this in the South Africa I lived in before I moved to England. Salaries for child-minders, their rights to holidays, pensions and so on have all now altered. People of different races are mixing together, but much of the infrastructure is deteriorating. For example, there are potholes in roads that were previously well maintained. The new policy of 'affirmative action' means that government jobs are now always allocated to black people first.

Personally, I acknowledge that change was necessary, although when there is change, something is always lost as well as gained. I am still able to return to my beautiful homeland and my wonderful family. I am now termed, I believe, as a 'scatterling' of Africa.

France

A personal account written by Yvonne Barry, now living in the South of France

When I was a child in Cannes it was a small town with sandy beaches, most of which you could go on free. There was one harbour, half of which was used by fishermen. There were three palaces (which later became hotels) and two casinos - one in winter and one in summer. There were a few grand villas on the hillside. It was a winter resort and you had to be rich to enjoy that kind of life.

There was no industry. The countryside around the town was taken up with the growing of flowers such as jasmine, rose and orange blossom for the manufacture of perfumes in the next town of Grasse. We lived in the grounds of one of the villas, my step-mother being housekeeper there.

Most people then were employed either in the hotels and large houses or in growing flowers and vegetables. I walked to school like all my friends and stayed all day, Monday to Wednesday. Thursday was free but was taken up by religious instruction. Friday and Saturday we were back in school all day.

Now things have changed. Where there were villas and flower-growing fields, the space has been taken over by developers and blocks of apartments replace them. It is no longer a winter season resort, but people come all the year round. The population has increased manyfold and many tourists come in their summer holidays to enjoy the water sports and get a sun tan. Many of the beaches are now privately owned by restaurants and hotels. The harbour only houses half a dozen fishing boats; the rest of the space has been taken over by pleasure yachts. The demand for leisure boating is so great that a new harbour had to be built.

The changes have created many more jobs and on the positive side the majority of people live better. But on the down side, it is no longer the quiet little town of years ago.

The Growth in Ownership of the Private Car
A personal account by Eileen Peck, born in England 1939, written February 2002

When I was a child in South London, the small number of cars on the road meant we could play out in the street and could walk to school alone, when we were only about seven years old, without fear of being run over. It also meant that our annual holiday (to Ramsgate) involved a journey by steam train and that if we went to visit relatives (which was rare) we went on the tram, bus or trolley bus.

By 1950 – when I was 11 – we acquired our first family car, which was a Rover. I remember that the car was our family's pride and joy - gleaming black with a magnificent wooden dashboard and running boards. The car was powered by petrol which was the common fuel for domestic cars, although lorries usually used diesel. Dad used to start it with a starting handle at the front. When John and I got married Dad gave us an old Austin 8, but when we bought our first house we could not afford to run a car so we managed for a year without one at all.

When we eventually got round to buying a car in the late 1960s, the roads were still very inadequate and a journey to John's sister - about 100 miles away - would take us almost four hours. This was halved to two hours by 2000. A visit to John's family in Borehamwood, the other side of London and about 45 miles away, would take over two hours - just an hour by the 1990s.

For some years John and I were a two-car family, but when we retired we sold one of them. It is not uncommon these days for a family to have three or four cars. During the last decade of the 20th century there was a huge increase in the number of very large cars called 'people carriers', which would take up to nine people. Four-wheel drive cars also became very popular - in these the driver and passengers were very high up and it was said that women liked driving them because they felt less intimidated by other drivers. This was important because 'road rage' (when frustrated drivers get aggressive, e.g. during a traffic jam) was a relatively new phenomenon on the roads at the turn of the century.

Because the majority of houses built before the time of mass car ownership do not have garages, most people, especially in towns, park out on the road. It is not uncommon for somebody to be unable to find a parking space on the road outside their own home and to have to park their car some distance away from where they live.

Many people, including myself, consider that late 20th century society has had to pay a high price for this ease of getting around. Campaigners claim that the motor car has brought about the destruction of huge areas of the countryside as well as largely destroying local communities. Children no longer play out in the streets as they used to do and we are suffering an increased incidence of asthma and other 'pollution related' illnesses. Road accident figures continue to be very high. There are forecasts of global warming because car emissions are contributing to a depletion of ozone in the atmosphere. Some experts predict that this will raise the temperature of the Earth, resulting in sea levels rising, the flooding of huge areas of land, and mass deaths. This process is already beginning - temperatures are higher than when I was a child. Future generations - who will hopefully have found less-intrusive and less-damaging ways of getting around - will probably be amazed that we allowed the motor car to dominate our lives in such a way!

The facts

- In 1900 the world was largely horse-drawn, although trains had already been around for over 50 years and were travelling at around 54 miles an hour. As the 20th century drew to a close, it was not uncommon for trains to cruise at 160 miles per hour, and those who travel by jet plane will be moving at something like 500 miles per hour.

- After the First World War there were around 186,000 private cars on the road in Great Britain. In 1936 this had risen to 2.5 million, and the figure in 1999 was close to 21 million. In 1998 American car factories turned out almost 7 million passenger cars in one year.

Crossing Borders in Europe

**A personal account written by Gert Been who lives in
The Netherlands**

1950s

In the fifties I lived as a child in Rotterdam in a small four room flat on
the third floor. My father had a cycle with a small engine connected to
the front wheel. With this cycle I made my first trip with my father
abroad. On a pleasant Sunday morning my father took me on the back
of the cycle and we travelled to the Belgian border, about 60km from
Rotterdam. At the border there was a red and white painted barrier
with a uniformed customs officer. We showed our passports. He looked
in our bags to see that we did not have butter or any other contraband
with us. At last he opened the barrier and for the first time in my life I
was in a foreign country. At a bureau de change we changed some
money to buy postcards to send to my grandfather and we bought some
real Belgian chocolate to take home. Late at night we returned,
satisfied, after our world tour!

1960s

In the late sixties, on a freezing December night, the train from
Rotterdam to Prague crawled along to the German-Czechoslovak border.
I was on my way to spend Christmas with a Czech friend I had met on an
international youth camp in East Mersey, England.

In the middle of nowhere the train stood still on a brightly-lit spot.
Billboards welcomed us to the Czechoslovak Socialist Republic. Other
billboards shouted protests against German imperialism. Armed soldiers
surrounded the train, and dark-looking border officers mounted the

carriages. Everybody in the train was quiet and frightened. The soldiers' dogs were barking continuously. Our passports were meticulously checked. 'Are your visas valid? How long are you going to stay here? What do you have with you? The newspaper you have with you is not allowed here – please give it to me! Open your bag! Now you must change your money. Write down the number of your camera. Don't forget to show yourself at the police station in Prague within 24 hours.' After three hours at border control, a steam locomotive started to pull our cold train to Prague through the darkness. Twenty-six hours later, we arrived in Prague. On the platform we pulled into were standing hundreds of Russian soldiers waiting for their train home to the USSR.

1990s

After an easy trip in the early spring, without stopping at any border, my family and I travelled through the former East Germany towards the Czech Republic. We passed the border in a few minutes; we were not even asked to show our passports. Our children did not seem to appreciate the significance for me of such an easy entry to the Czech Republic. For them there are no borders in Europe any more. The Czech side of the border, formerly a closed agricultural world, was now a red-light district with dozens of long-legged, sparsely clothed girls waiting to be picked up.

From Local Shops to Out-of-town Supermarkets
A personal account by Eileen Peck, born in England 1939

1940s

In the 1940s we did all our shopping in Norwood High Street in South London. This was a short walk from home. Mum would push me down the traffic-free hill in my pram, on top of which was the 'bag wash': a large pillowcase into which were stuffed our bed sheets and towels to be taken to the laundry. After the laundry, the first stop was the Co-operative shop where we bought 'groceries'. The shop smelled of a mixture of soap and bacon. Down one side was a huge wooden counter along the front of which, at a child's head height, glass-topped square biscuit tins were arranged at a slight angle to allow a view of the contents. Biscuits were weighed out into paper bags. Most of the goods were weighed out rather than pre-packed. When mum handed over her cash (no credit cards were used then), the assistant put the money into a small round container which was clipped onto a wire and then whisked up to the ceiling and across the shop to a cubicle in the corner. Here a cashier handled the money and returned the change. I remember that because of wartime rationing we only had pretty basic foods and the prices always remained the same. It was not until some years after the war that price controls were lifted and inflation took over. After the Co-op we went to the greengrocer, the baker and the butcher. Mum had the difficult task of carrying all the goods home in shopping bags piled on top of the pram.

1960s

In the 1960s, when my children were young, their experience of shopping was very different. We would go by car to a supermarket that was within easy driving distance. These early supermarkets were quite small and were often part of national chains. The goods they sold were generally identical in branches throughout the UK. We could, however, also do some shopping in small shops locally. When we moved out of London to a village, in 1964, there was quite a large collection of shops, each run by a private individual. There was a butcher's shop, a fishmongers/fish and chip shop, two greengrocers, a hardware shop, a shop selling electrical appliances, two pharmacies, two newsagents, a haberdasher's, a general grocery store, a jeweller's shop, two ladies' wear shops and a baker's. You could buy virtually all you needed from these local shops.

1990s

By the 1990s supermarkets had become much larger and by then their range also included cosmetics and pharmacy products and, in some branches, clothing, household goods and even furniture. In fact, they boasted that they sold everything you needed for the home under one roof: one-stop shopping. Most products were heavily packaged so that vast trolleys piled high with food would be trundled out of the store and packed into the boot of the car. We now have one supermarket a mile away, another two miles away, and a third about three miles away.

2000

By 2000 most of our local food shops had been replaced. The only ones that remained were the bakery (with few customers and struggling to make a profit), a general grocery store, the haberdasher, one pharmacy and one newsagent. The others have been replaced by: a betting shop, an Indian restaurant and take-away, a kebab house, a pizzeria, three hairdressers and two estate agents. There is now much more of an emphasis on providing a service rather than goods. Although there is now far more choice in what we buy, I feel we have lost something very special with the demise of small independently-owned shops. Walking to the local shops, as we often did, gave us the opportunity to meet up with and chat to neighbours. We also got to know, quite well sometimes, the people who owned and worked in the shops. Supermarkets feel less friendly and we don't have the same opportunities to meet up with friends. I know lots of my friends feel the same. I wonder whether in years to come people will be saying, 'Do you mean individuals used to be able to open their own shop?'

21st century

By the beginning of the 21st century the major supermarkets had introduced shopping on the Internet. My children, now living in London with busy careers and homes of their own to maintain, often order through the Internet and have the goods delivered for just £5. I have heard that houses are now being built with a special collection unit that is equipped to receive the weekly shopping – with a freezer compartment and a chilled area. Perhaps, at some time in the future, all shopping will be done 'online' and going out shopping will be a thing of the past. This will save a lot of time, but our sense of community will decline even more with no opportunity for socialising while shopping.

Telephones - Then and Now
A personal account written by Lesley Barry of Chalkwell, Essex, in England

1960s

We never had a telephone when I lived at home with my parents in the 1960s. Communicating with anyone who did not live on our estate meant using the public telephone box. There were two within reasonable walking distance, although one had a distinct advantage over the other - it was close to the launderette, so if it was being used, one could lurk around in the soapy warmth until it became vacant.

My Dad taught me to use the telephone when I was about six. It was still Button A and Button B in those days and one had to be trained. I seem to remember that it cost about two old pennies (1p) to make a call. Not that we had to do it very often - we did not know many people who had a phone.

1970s

As we moved into the 1970s and I entered into my teenage years, the telephone box became much more a part of my life. Many more people had private phones and, as has happened for generations, the youth of the day were quick to embrace this now more accessible technology. If you were lucky, you might get a boyfriend whose parents had a phone and would let him use it. But it was still possible to find people who didn't or couldn't. Oh, the agony of trying to conduct a teenage romance using public phones! The contact hour and place had to be planned with military precision, and the subterfuge that had to be practised in order not to set parental antennae quivering. Our dog had never been for so many walks!

At the appointed hour one would sally forth to make the all-important call. No point in going too early because the call could not be made until the appointed minute, but one mustn't be late or he might have gone home again. So, with heart beating at an increasingly fast rate, one would approach the phone box. Would there be someone in there already? This was particularly worrying if one was to be the 'phonee' rather than the 'phoner'. Would he have already rung and you'd missed the call? What if you were in the box waiting for the call to come through and an adult turned up and wanted to use the phone? You could not pick up the receiver and pretend to be on a call because your caller would get an engaged tone. Agony, agony. Good manners dictated that one had to leave the kiosk and let the grown-up make their call whilst praying that a) it would be a very short call and not overrun your appointed time and b) that the 'phoner', having tried and got an engaged tone, would keep trying until you were able to pick up. If all went to plan and one finally did get to talk, you would hardly be through the platitudes before the pips would go, signifying the end of the call, and putting an end to the sweet nothings composed on the interminable journey to the phone box, leaving nothing for it but to trudge home again, only to go through the entire gamut of emotions the following evening.

21st century

Now, of course, in the 21st century, youngsters don't know they are born. They blithely master all the communications technology available to them and appear to own at least three mobile phones each. They can leave messages, text each other, find out who called them while they were out, and talk to each other at any time of the day or night, without a by-your-leave to anyone.

My own mother now has not only a private telephone, but a mobile phone and an answering machine, which of course I spend most of my filial-duty time talking to. My five year old daughter, asked to write a book for World Book Day, came up with her own version of 'Goldilocks and the Three Bears' which had Goldilocks phoning the three bears on Daddy Bear's mobile to tell them that the porridge was now the correct temperature.

Is all this increased access to other people a good thing? Difficult to say. We are all grateful to the mobile phone when we can ring for an ambulance to be at the next station when someone has a heart attack on the train, but don't we all get a little tired of hearing the question, 'Hello, where are you? What time will you be home?'

Information Technology

A personal account by Eileen Peck, born in England 1939, written February 2002

When I was a child there were no automated telephone exchanges. You simply asked the telephonist for every number and she would put you through. We did not have a telephone in our house until I was 21. There was no email and if you wanted to get a written message delivered quickly you filled in a 'telegram' form at the Post Office and it would be delivered by a telegram boy, often on a bicycle.

Each book in a public library had a card inside and each library member had a small envelope in the library filing system. When I chose a book the card was transferred from the book to my own small envelope so that the library had a record of who had which books. When I was about 50, public libraries first started to use computers to keep their records.

When I was a child, shops had manual cash registers. The shop assistant would press keys representing the cost and this would mechanically open the till drawer and a bell would ring. No receipt was issued and if you wanted a receipt it would be written on a pad by hand. We did not have a bank account until I was in my late 20s - all payments then were made by cash. There were no credit cards.

When I started work in a solicitor's office there were no computers - only typewriters. If I had to type a Will I had to make sure I made not one single mistake as Wills had to be typed perfectly. If I did make a mistake I had to start again. How wonderful when word processors came along!

By the time I was middle-aged we, like many of our friends, had two computers. We were connected to the Internet on which we became increasingly dependent for banking, shopping, booking holidays, theatre trips and lots of other things. Businesses depended on computers. The introduction of automatic telephone answering by businesses was very frustrating and we often yearned to hear the sound of a human voice to get the answer to a question for which the computer was not programmed.

The facts

- In 1946, IBM introduced the 'electronic brain'. It could do calculations at lightning speed and with it came the beginning of a whole new language with terms like 'memory' and 'programming'. It was said that eventually everyone would be using electronic calculators for everyday tasks.

- In 1954, IBM introduced their first business computer. In 1958 came the silicon chip which led to the miniaturisation of computers, and by 1982 the word processor hit the business world.

- Imperial, Britain's last major typewriter manufacturer, closed in 1975.

- During the 1980s there was a massive growth in computer use in business and by the end of the century computers were moving into domestic use.

- At the British General Election in 1997 Tony Blair, leader of the Labour Party, promised a computer in every classroom. When he became Prime

Minister he also offered free computer training for adults because he said that as a nation Britain must become computer literate.

Housing, Daily Life and Personal Hygiene
A personal account written by Maria van Donkelaar, living in the Netherlands

As a result of the Second World War bombing in Rotterdam there was a severe housing shortage in 1947, the year I was born. My family - my father, mother, grandmother and I - occupied the bedroom floor of a small apartment.

Every Friday evening we took our weekly bath. There was no shower, bath or warm running water. We heated water-filled saucepans on the gas stove. The floor was covered by a large plastic sheet on which a tub was placed. It was big enough for me but the adults of the family could only just about sit in it. The boiling water was emptied into the tub and made up to the right temperature by adding cold water.

Sometimes after my bath I was given a cup of clear broth, which my mother would have prepared for the weekend soup, or in winter I might have been given hot chocolate. After that it was on with the clean clothes and to bed. It was quite time-consuming and was almost like a ritual.

In 1975 I lived on my own in an old apartment in the same city. Times had changed. For civilised citizens, showers had become a necessary part of life. In the hallway the previous inhabitant had had a shower built into a cupboard space adjoining the loo. You entered the shower via the toilet, which was separated by a plastic curtain. I seem to remember that the whole space covered about two square metres. It was not exactly the lap of luxury by modern standards, but I was very pleased with this facility.

Now, in 2002, my youngest son, who is 13 years old, has just told me that his longest record for taking a shower stands at 45 minutes. These days I often shower in the morning as well as in the evening, or at the end of a busy day I might relax in the bath for half an hour.

I could tell you a similar story about washing clothes. Think about how it must have been when I was young for my mother to do the washing without warm running water. Needless to say it was an activity that took up most of the day, every Monday. Later, around 1960, my mother won a radio quiz and received as a prize a 'quick washer'. It was a large piece of apparatus with a mangle (a device with rollers for wringing out the water from clothes) which was collected from the shed (in the meantime we had moved to a farm) and put in the kitchen on the same waterproof sheet. Today we do a quick wash. Or rather we hardly do anything, it is the machine that does it all, fully automatic. What an increase in water consumption in comparison to my younger days.

RECORDING CHANGES IN YOUR LIFETIME

What Events were Significant for You?

Headline events in the outside world will impact to a greater or lesser degree on each individual. An obvious example is the Second World War. If you happened to be living in a small village during the war years and your father was not conscripted, the impact of the war is likely to have been far less traumatic than if you had, for example, lived in London, been evacuated and possibly orphaned, when your father was killed in action. Similarly, the terrorist attack on the World Trade Centre on September 11, 2001 will certainly be remembered by everyone, but if you were living in a remote village in say, rural France, then the impact will have been much less than if you were living in Manhattan and had a relative or friend who died in the disaster.

On the other hand, relatively small events - which may not have made their way into the papers - might be very significant and important to you personally. The opening of your parish's new church hall, for which you had spent years raising funds, might be one such example.

How then can you best capture something of the events that were significant to you during your lifetime? How can you paint for your descendants the historical backcloth against which your life is being played out? Three approaches which you could consider are:

- Reportage
- A timeline
- Memory notes

Any of these could be included in your 'alternative' autobiography.

Reportage

Reportage is a useful approach for recording headline-making national, or even international events, but it also has a part to play in recording everyday events which are important to you and your family. For example, your reportage account of your wedding day would no doubt be very interesting to your descendants. An account of the day a grandchild was born would be especially interesting to that grandchild.

Reportage has a central place in history. It gives a sense of authenticity to events which is often absent from accounts based on research. The fact that reportage depends on an individual being able to write (or having someone on hand who can write for them) has meant that prior to the late 19th century, when widespread education started to become available in many countries, reportage was almost exclusively dominated by those in positions of privilege in society.

If a particular event has had a great impact on you, you could write a 'reportage' account giving your own perspective on what happened, how you were involved, and how you felt at the time. For example, you might think that you could give a good account of the events that surrounded the death of Princess Diana or you might have very clear memories of an amazing night out at a concert - perhaps when the Beatles or the Three Tenors were performing. Perhaps you went on peace marches, possibly anti-Vietnam. You could choose to describe how you heard the news of the assassination of President Kennedy. Or you could describe how you welcomed in the new Millennium.

Reportage cannot be considered as an absolutely objective account of what happened. However objective eyewitnesses think they are being, they cannot help bringing their own perspective to the event. Reportage reflects the eyewitness's prejudices and beliefs. If you were to compare accounts of an event written by several different people they would not be exactly the same. This is a phenomenon well-known to the police, who often get conflicting accounts of what happened following a road accident! If you decide to write a reportage account of an event as part of your 'Gift', all you can hope for is to be as honest as you can. Value judgements are okay - they will say a lot about you to future generations - but resist the temptation to embellish the facts.

If you find writing difficult, you could make an audio recording of your reportage account. You could then make a typescript copy of the content so that if the cassette gets lost or damaged the written account will survive.

Whether you are writing (or recording) an account of a great national event or a small family celebration, a good starting point would be to make some notes giving a rough outline of what you want to say. You might like to include some of the following:

- The name of the event with date and place
- Who was with you
- What you wore
- The weather
- A description of the venue
- How many people attended
- What happened
- A description of the principal people who took part
- How you felt on the day - were you excited, sad, overwhelmed or even frightened?
- How the event affected you afterwards

To help you get started, consider the following reportage account.

Report of the Day of Princess Diana's Funeral at Westminster Abbey

My friend Mia and I were both so sad at the death of Princess Diana that we decided to go to London for the funeral. We started out from home very early - just after 6am - and made our way to the railway station. We were both wearing black suits with white blouses and had each bought a bouquet of flowers. As we neared the station we met up with lots of other people, mostly women, who were also going into London for the funeral. It was a bright and sunny day. As we boarded the train we were surprised to see that it was so crowded. Nearly every seat was taken and the majority of people were women, although there were also some family groups with young children.

Many were dressed in dark colours and were holding flowers, and they were all chatting in a very animated way. Although we were all going to a funeral everyone seemed quite 'high' - perhaps it was a reaction, a way of dealing with our feelings.

Following the death of Princess Diana in a car crash in Paris, the media had been full of stories of her life. She was regarded by many people as very beautiful and it was said that she brought a 'breath of fresh air' to the monarchy. Because of her very natural approach when she visited patients suffering from Aids and those living in poverty in Britain and abroad, many considered her quite saintly. The nation had been swept by great emotion after her death. Some saw it as a sort of mass hysteria, but my friend Mia and I felt we knew and loved her and wanted to say our 'Goodbyes' at the funeral.

We were on the pavement just outside Westminster Abbey when the police horses came into view. I guess they were there to control the crowds but they had a very easy day because everyone was very orderly. As the hearse with the coffin approached a great hush went over the crowd. Everyone was so quiet - lost in their own thoughts. My heart went out to Princes William and Harry, Princess Diana's two young sons, who looked so sad and lonely. They were walking so sombrely behind their mother's coffin. I felt I would like to have been able to give them a hug. And why wasn't Prince Charles at least putting his arm round the young boy, Harry? I guess the royal family aren't allowed to do that sort of thing. That's just what Princess Diana found so difficult - she was such a touchy-feely person. There was a small bunch of flowers with the word 'Mummy' on top of the coffin.

We saw the Queen arrive and then watched the ceremony on a huge television screen that had been erected outside the Abbey.

As the service progressed the crowd was absolutely silent. You could have heard a pin drop! But then, a round of applause started and drifted through the crowd until there was uproar! That was a remarkable spontaneous reaction to the speech of Earl Spencer, Princess Diana's brother. I was so pleased I went to London that day. I felt very close to Princess Diana. It was good to be able to say a proper goodbye to the 'People's Princess'.

A Timeline

If you don't want to spend too much time recording events that have happened during your lifetime, you might like to draw a timeline. Educationalists often use timelines to help to clarify the relationship between different events. In your case it will show what was happening to you in your life when particular events were happening in the world. This will help to put your life in its historical context and will be interesting to your descendants. Include events that were important and significant to you as well as those which you think your descendants will have heard of. Timelines can be written either vertically or horizontally, the former being much easier to accomplish using a computer. A useful source of information here is the *Chronicle of the 20th Century* (see Appendix 1). You can also access material on the Internet - just search for 'timeline' and you will discover lots of interesting websites.

The following example shows what such a timeline might look like:

World Events	Year	Joan Brown, née Smith - Life Events
World War II begins	1939	Born in London
	1944	Started school
US drops atomic bombs on Japan	1945	
State of Israel founded	1948	
First modern credit card introduced	1950	
Princess Elizabeth becomes Queen at age 25	1952	
	1953	Moved to Cambridge
	1956	Left school and started work
Berlin Wall built	1961	
	1962	Married John Brown in Cambridge
JFK assassinated	1963	Moved back to London
	1964	First son (Harry) born
US sends troops to Vietnam	1965	Moved to Southend-on-Sea
First heart transplant	1967	Second son (Tom) born
Neil Armstrong becomes first man on the Moon	1969	
	1970	Daughter (Katie) born
	1971	John started working for XYZ Company
	1978	Started degree course in London
Margaret Thatcher becomes British Prime Minister	1979	
	1984	Started teaching at XYZ College
Hole in the ozone layer discovered	1985	
Official end of the Cold War	1992	
Channel Tunnel opens, connecting Britain and France	1994	
US President Bill Clinton impeachment proceedings	1998	
	1999	John retired from work
	2000	First grandson (Joseph Byron) born
Terrorists attack World Trade Centre in New York	2001	

Memory Notes

A third approach would be to make a few notes about significant events that happened during your lifetime. You could consider these notes as shortened reportage accounts. They could be added to your 'alternative' autobiographical writings. Anything that evokes powerful memories is worth recording. The important thing is to try to include something of how the event affected you personally, how you felt at the time. Remember, too, that you could make an audio recording instead of a written account.

Second World War

Most people who were alive during the Second World War, even if they were very young, have a tale to tell. It is such personal stories that would bring to life for future generations a period that would otherwise be just a string of historical facts. Stories might be of action in the front line, the difficulty of trying to feed a family on a very limited ration, or of young women partying with foreign servicemen based temporarily in their country.

Space

The second half of the 20th century was truly the time when man left the Earth's atmosphere for the first time and reached for the stars (even though he has so far only stepped onto the Moon!). Perhaps your descendants in 100 years time will be able to travel in space themselves. They will surely be interested to hear your account of watching, on the television, man's first steps into space in 1969.

The Monarchy

If you live in a monarchy you could write some notes about the coronation of a king or queen, or some other royal occasion.

Currency Changes

How did you adjust when the old currency gave way to the new?

Sport

Have you any outstanding sporting memories to record? Perhaps you went to the Olympic Games and were present when a world record was broken? Perhaps you even competed. The football World Cup would be another sporting event worth reporting on, especially if your team won!

Entertainment

Could you reminisce about dancing in the cinemas when Bill Haley and the Comets hit the cinema screen? Did you swoon at a concert of The Beatles or Madonna? What did you think of Michael Jackson and his make-up?

Politics

If you've been involved as a participant in or interested observer of the political scene you might like to write about your experiences. Perhaps you belonged to a political party and went to (or spoke at) a party conference. Perhaps you campaigned in a Presidential election. Perhaps you went on the anti-Vietnam marches. Were you an anti-roads campaigner? Did you campaign for equal rights in the USA?

There were lots of events during the second half of the 20th century which you could comment on. Remember to say how you felt and how the event affected you and your family. Give your opinion on what was going on. For instance, you could write a short piece on:

- The Cuban missile crisis
- The building (1963) or dismantling (1989) of the Berlin Wall
- Nelson Mandela's release from gaol in South Africa
- The atomic bombs dropped on Japan in 1945
- The assassination of President John F Kennedy in 1962
- The crisis at Little Rock, USA, in the mid-1950s
- The Vietnam War
- The opening of Disneyland in 1955
- The opening of the first McDonald's in 1955
- The change to decimal currency in the UK
- The Oklahoma City bombing

If you would like to remind yourself of some of the events that have happened during your lifetime a good starting point is the

Chronicle of the 20th Century, which is a collection of newspaper accounts of events all over the world. Or, again, just search the Internet which has lots of useful websites.

To Sum Up

• Commenting on events that have happened during your lifetime will help your descendants to see your life in a historical context.

• Use reportage, a timeline or memory notes to make-up or add to an 'alternative' autobiography.

• Be sure to give a personal perspective - How did you feel? What did you do?

LOOKING TO THE FUTURE

Having spent some time thinking about how the world has changed and is changing during your lifetime, you can now have some fun thinking about what changes might occur in the future. Science fiction often presents us with ideas of how the world will look in years to come, but the question is - what do you think? Just for fun, let your imagination fly and spend some time recording your thoughts on how you see the world in say, 100 years from now.

- Will Man have stepped onto another planet?
- Will cancer have been conquered?
- Will everyone be working a three-day week?
- Will we be travelling around in cars that drive themselves?
- What will our homes be like?
- Will euthanasia be legal in many countries?
- What will our clothes be like?
- Will we be on the way to a world government?
- How will nations be resolving disputes - will they still be fighting wars?
- Will you be able to 'buy' a clone of yourself to replace you when you die?

Your projections about the future, if you record them now, could provide great entertainment when they are read out at a family gathering 100 years from now. Will your descendants be filled with amazement at the accuracy of your predictions or enjoy a good laugh because they were way off the mark? It could be fun for you to speculate and it will certainly be fun for your descendants to read about your ideas.

If the idea of thinking about and predicting the future appeals to you, you could 'cheat' by getting some pointers from William Davis's *The Lucky Generation*. His very positive view of the future makes predictions covering a wide range of social trends and developments.

The point is - what do *you* think? It is your views that will interest your descendants. But this will only happen if you take a short time to record your thoughts and predictions now.

PART VII

PRESERVATION

ABOUT PRESERVATION

However much work you put into creating your Gift, it could be lost unless you give some attention to preserving the finished work. Because the aim here is to preserve your Gift so it will last as far into the future as possible, try to make the finished package compact and durable. That is, it should not take up too much space and should be able to stand the stresses and strains of time. However, don't spend too much time worrying about the longevity of your Gift. It's better to produce something than to become so inhibited by worries about whether it will last that you produce nothing!

You may be wondering how long you can realistically expect your Gift to last. Although it is never possible to say that something will last 'X' number of years – even if it is kept in optimum conditions – you can strive to eliminate as many of the potential hazards as possible, in order to arrest the decay and prolong the 'life' of the artefact. Your descendants will thank you for taking the trouble.

Whatever form your Gift takes, it will stand a better chance of surviving into the future if you give thought to the following issues.

The Materials you Use

Some materials and artefacts are far more durable than others. Do not assume that newer technologies ensure longevity. Some old sepia photographs have withstood time better than some more modern colour photographs. Digitally stored records will not necessarily have a long life - there is still uncertainty about their durability.

Archival-quality materials will almost certainly not be available in your local shopping mall, but can be got from specialist suppliers, some of which are listed in Appendix 2.

A letter can easily be written or printed onto acid-free paper, slipped into an archival-quality polyester sleeve and then stored in a box in the conditions described below.

A journal, if you use word processing, could be treated in a similar fashion, perhaps with each polyester sleeve filed away into a folder which is then housed in a box.

If you are producing a Life Book, again, try to use only archival-quality materials including adhesives and mounting corners. Some non-photographic items, like newspaper cuttings and postcards, could be put into separate protective sleeves so that any photo-destructive qualities they have are isolated.

Storage Conditions

Whatever form your Gift takes, be it a Life Photo Album, a Treasure Box or some written material, you will slow down its deterioration if you keep it in an environment that is cool - between 18-21°C - and dry and stable. This will not necessarily be easy because modern houses are usually centrally heated and sometimes air conditioned, which will create a hot and dry environment that will cause wood to crack and paper to become brittle. The best places are usually in a bedroom, a hallway or a dining room because these are likely to have a more constant and lower temperature. Cellars are often damp, while attics can fluctuate in temperature considerably, often becoming very hot in summer.

Be careful to look out for places within the chosen room that might cause a problem. Damp spots on a wall, tiled floors which will get cold, and draughty corners should all be avoided, as should areas near to windows (because of strong light) and anywhere near heating and air-conditioning appliances.

If you are really serious about protecting your material, there are some simple devices to measure humidity on the market, and you could also decide to invest in a minimum/maximum thermometer.

Prolonged exposure to light, especially strong sunlight, should be avoided, but this need not be a problem if your Gift is stored in a box of some kind.

You might be interested in conducting a simple experiment to see how the materials you use can deteriorate under adverse light conditions. Take some examples (not precious originals!) of the materials you are using, such as a page of written or printed text, a photograph, a newspaper cutting, a picture printed on your inkjet printer etc. and pin them onto a board placed where they will get a lot of sunlight. Keep an identical set in more ideal storage conditions. After, say, six months, make a comparison between the two sets to see just how much deterioration has occurred.

Professional conservators regularly inspect their archived materials - you might care to do the same. While on the subject of professional conservators, do be sure to approach the conservator at your local museum if you need advice - they are usually very helpful.

Ensure that the Gift is Recognised as Something Important to be Passed On

Remember that as well as using suitable materials and finding a suitable storage place for your Gift, it is important to ensure that people are able to identify just how important your package is. It will need to jump out at them from among other possessions to ensure that it does not end up at the local charity shop after your death (or the death of one of your descendants).

The best way to ensure that your descendants are able to identify your Gift as something important is to package it very attractively. If you do so, it is more likely that the Gift will be kept out on display, perhaps in the living-room, rather than hidden away in a corner of the attic. This will have three benefits: it is more likely to be kept at an even temperature and humidity, which will help preserve it; it will be enjoyed by interested people; and it is more likely to be identified as something important when the owner dies and his or her things are being sorted out. A disadvantage of allowing your Gift to be on display is that it would suffer from frequent handling. Fingerprints (which leave damaging traces of oil), and tiny creases and tears will take their toll over the years. This could be alleviated by encouraging anyone wanting to inspect the material to wear a pair of fine gloves, which could be kept either with it or close by.

Care should also be taken with labelling so that it is clear who the Gift is from. A very effective way of doing this is to include a simple family tree identifying yourself within the family structure.

You will, of course, make sure that your own immediate family members know of the existence of your Gift. You might like to bequeath it in your Will. This will be especially important if you have no close relatives but want the Gift to be handed to a more distant relation.

To Sum Up

• Don't let worries about how long your Gift will last prevent you from producing something.
• Use archival-quality materials.
• Keep your Gift in the most favourable storage conditions.
• If possible, keep your Gift on display.
• Ensure people take care when handling your Gift.
• Ensure your Gift is carefully labelled, preferably including a simple family.

PART VIII

INFORMATION SHEETS

FACTUAL INFORMATION SHEETS

These *Information Sheets* have been provided so that you can easily produce a structured account of the facts of your life. It may be that you have covered some of the subjects in the *Information Sheets* elsewhere. For example, some of the names and dates will be in your family tree and the section on Health could be covered in your 'alternative' autobiography. These *Information Sheets* are self-contained and give you an opportunity to record the nuts and bolts of your life so far and to make it easy to continue updating the information in the future. You can also record any information you have about your ancestors. The sheets, especially if combined with a few carefully labelled photographs, would in themselves make a very informative Gift. They could also be used to consolidate information in any other part of your Gift.

It may not be possible to complete every section in these sheets. For instance, your knowledge of your grandparents might be very limited. Don't worry about this. Just be assured that any work you do to preserve information you have NOW will help family historians in the future. Try to fill in as much of the sheets as possible. It's surprising how just reading the sheets and concentrating on particular events or places can stimulate your memory, and you could find that at a moment when you least expect it - often when you wake in the morning - a previously 'lost' memory will come to you.

The *Information Sheets* have been completed with the 'average' family in mind, although recent years have brought about huge changes in the types of family composition. The 'norm' now includes several marriages, single parent families, children born out of wedlock and families that include step and foster relationships.

As always, ensure that the material survives into the future by choosing good archival-quality materials. A specialist company would supply acid-free paper onto which you could copy the sheets, polyester sleeves into which each sheet could then be slipped, and a folder to keep the sheets together.

You should enlarge the sheets to 155% when you photocopy them.

FACTUAL INFORMATION SHEET

Information Sheet for the Life of:

Full name	
Latest address	
Date of birth	Place of birth

Immediate Lineage - state whether birth-child, fostered or adopted

Father's full name	
Latest address	
Occupation	
Date of birth	Date of death
Place of birth	Place of death

Mother's full name	
Latest address	
Occupation	
Date of birth	Date of death
Place of birth	Place of death

Paternal Grandfather's full name	
Latest address	
Occupation	
Date of birth	Date of death
Place of birth	Place of death

Immediate Lineage *continued*

Paternal Grandmother's *full name*	
Latest address	
Occupation	
Date of birth	*Date of death*
Place of birth	*Place of death*

Maternal Grandfather's *full name*	
Latest address	
Occupation	
Date of birth	*Date of death*
Place of birth	*Place of death*

Maternal Grandmother's *full name*	
Latest address	
Occupation	
Date of birth	*Date of death*
Place of birth	*Place of death*

Enter any other significant information you know about your immediate forebears (including, if appropriate, where they are buried).

Early Years

Position in family	
Names of siblings	
First address	
First memory	
Any other significant information about your early years - favourite toy, food, clothes etc.	

Childhood Experiences

Describe your family home (e.g. sleeping, cooking arrangements etc).
Describe the area in which you lived.
How did you spend your time when not in school?
Say something about family life (e.g. holidays and birthday celebrations).
How did your family celebrate Christmas or any other festivals?
Enter any other significant memories / information about your childhood (include changes such as when the family bought their first TV or car).

Early Schooling

At what age did you start school?
What was your first school?
What were your favourite lessons / games / activities / books / foods etc?
Include any other memories / significant information, e.g. pocket money, special treats etc.

Later Schooling

Names of other schools
Favourite lessons / games / activities
Any other memories / significant information (Saturday job?)

Education After Compulsory Schooling

How old were you when you left school?
Did you go on to any further or higher education or training immediately, or later in life? Where?
What did you study?
Any other memories / significant information about leaving school.

Early Adult Years

How old were you when you left home?
Where did you go to live?
What did you do in your spare time?
Any other memories / significant information about your early adult years.

Working Life

How old were you when you started work?
What was your first job?
How much did you earn?
Any other memories / significant information about your working life.
List the jobs you have had (a CV or résumé would be interesting).

Later Training/Education

Did you return to education later in life (perhaps evening classes)?
Any other memories/significant information about later training/education.

First Marriage[3]

How did you meet your partner?
How old were you, and your partner?
Did you marry and, if so, give date.
Partner's name
Where was your first home together?
Names and dates of birth of any children from this relationship.
How long was this relationship?
If it ended, why? (e.g. divorce/death of partner)
Any memories/information about your years in this relationship.

[3] For 'marriage' also read 'significant relationship of some duration'.

Subsequent Marriage(s)

How did you meet your partner?

How old were you, and your partner?

Did you marry and, if so, give date.

Partner's name

Where was your first home together?

Names and dates of birth of any children from this relationship.

How long was this relationship?

If it ended, why? (e.g. divorce / death of partner)

Any memories / information about your years in this relationship.

Children

Children's names.

List any memories of their personalities and exploits during their childhood years. It is helpful to record your children's earliest years because their own recall of this period will be very limited.

Interests/Pastimes

List your hobbies.

Describe those things that you feel make life worthwhile, and give you pleasure.

Other information not covered above.

Health

Briefly describe the general state of your health and that of immediate family members.

THOUGHTS & FEELINGS
INFORMATION SHEETS

Warning - Approach with Care!

This is where the work can get very interesting, and many people would find this part of their ancestors' lives the most compelling. Wouldn't you like to have access to your ancestors' innermost thoughts and feelings? If so, then you can assume that your descendants will be fascinated by yours. The only way to make such information available to them is to record it now.

In focussing on your thoughts and feelings, consider how you see yourself and how you relate to those close to you and to the world in general. How you feel is reflected by (and some people think is determined by) the thoughts that you have. Would it surprise you if you discovered that your grandmother was just like you in that she tended to get bored very easily and always had to have something stimulating happening in her life? Or that again, just like you, she was a very sympathetic person who always liked to help anyone in need? Wouldn't it be interesting if you discovered that your grandparents' marriage was largely happy but was sometimes affected by battles for power, with a rather controlling husband (or wife) and a submissive wife (or husband) who was always trying to please? If this pattern reflected what happened in your own marriage, then this knowledge could be very illuminating.

How did you become the person you are? If you are dynamic and confident, were you born that way or did it result from the encouragement you received as a child? Were you placid as a baby or was that something that came from living in a tranquil and easy-going home? While it is true to say that there is still considerable dispute about the degree of influence of your genetic make-up and of the environment in which you were raised, lots of people in the fields of psychology, sociology and genetics have applied themselves to the question and have come up with some very interesting findings.

Cohort studies[4] have shown that certain personality traits present at birth remain into adult life. It was deduced that these traits can be genetically determined. It must be gratifying to psychologists that their findings have been supported by geneticists who have very recently identified genes responsible for a number of personality characteristics, such as placidity, shyness and curiosity. So we see that certain attributes can be passed down the generations in a particular family. Interesting indeed for our descendants!

Just a word of caution before you start: reflecting on your life and times in terms of thoughts and feelings may feel a little uncomfortable. After all, committing to paper aspects of your innermost thoughts and feelings can seem rather threatening. If, having acknowledged this, you decide that the project does interest you, and that you do want to pursue it, then you might like to have a friend or relative on hand to offer some support.

---

[4] This is where a group of people of a particular age are studied at intervals as they move through life.

THOUGHTS & FEELINGS INFORMATION SHEET

Completed by	Date

Early Family Life

Say something about your parents and their situation when you were born. How old were they? Were they materially comfortable or worried about money? What do you think their marriage relationship was like? Do you think you were a welcomed baby?

Did you have any siblings - what was your position in the family?

Describe the family 'ambience' into which you were born. Was it, for example, relaxed and carefree, or strict and repressive?

What lasting effect do you think the family 'ambience' had on you?

Childhood Years

Did you feel loved and valued as a child?

Describe the way in which you were disciplined, e.g. sent to your room, smacked or glared at.

If you were to have had a family 'motto' what would it be? (e.g. 'If at first you don't succeed, try, try, and try again.') State some of your family sayings.

If you were an only child, did this worry or please you?

Are there any aspects of your childhood that had a lasting effect on you?

Relationships

Say something about your relationship with your father.

Say something about your relationship with your mother.

Say something about your relationships with your siblings.

In what ways do you think these relationships influenced you?

Adult Life

How do you see yourself? Describe your personality, strengths and weaknesses.

What things make you happy?

Adult Life *continued*

What things make you anxious and worried?

What, if anything, would you like to change about yourself?

Do you feel emotionally/mentally stable? If not entirely, how do you feel that this gets in the way of your enjoyment of life?

Marriage Relationships

Say something about your marriage relationships in terms of who makes the decisions, how you resolve disputes, and what strengths and weaknesses you both have.

What are the things that you and your partner have in common? What do you enjoy together?

APPENDIX 1

Additional Reading

Green, Jonathon, *Dictionary of New Words*, Bloomsbury Publishing Ltd., 1991

Davis, William, *The Lucky Generation*, Headline, 1995

Kirschner Braun, Bev, *Crafting Your Own Heritage Album*, Better Way, 2000

Currer-Briggs, Noel, *Worldwide Family History*, Routledge & Kegan Paul, 1982

Cole, Jean, and Titford, John, *Tracing Your Family Tree*, Countryside Books, 2000

Pols, Robert, *Dating Old Photographs*, Countryside Books, 1992

Chisholm, Alison, and Courtie, Brenda, *How to Write about Yourself*, Allison & Busby Ltd., 1999

Explore your Family's Past, Readers Digest

Amsden, Peter C, *Images for the Future*, ASAT Productions, 2000

Powell Crowe, Elizabeth, *Genealogy on Line*, McGraw Hill, 2000

Rutledge Stephenson, Lynda, *The Complete Idiot's Guide to Writing Your Family History*, Alpha Books, 2000

Beal Steven, *The Complete Idiot's Guide to Making Home Videos*, Alpha Books, 2000

Hedgecoe, John, *Hedgecoe on Video: a Complete Creative & Technical Guide to Making Videos*, Mitchell Beazley, 1995

Chronicle of the 20th Century, Longman, 1988

Cameron, Julia, *The Artist's Way*, Souvenir Press Ltd., 1992

Humphreys, John, *The Great Food Gamble*, Hodder & Stoughton, 2001

APPENDIX 2

Useful Contacts and Addresses

Genealogical Research

British Library Oriental and India Office
Collections
96 Euston Road
London NW1 2DB
Phone: 020 7412 7873
www.bl.uk/collections/oriental

British Library Newspaper Library
Colindale Avenue
London NW9 5HE
Phone: 020 7412 7353
www.bl.uk/collections/newspaper

Catholic Central Library
Lancing Street
London NW1 1ND
Phone: 020 7383 4333
www.catholic-library.org.uk

Civil registration certificates
(applications by post)
Postal Application Section
Office for National Statistics
PO Box 2
Southport
Merseyside PR8 2JD
Phone: 0870 243 7788

College of Arms
Queen Victoria Street
London EC4V 4BT
Phone: 020 7248 2742
www.college-of-arms.gov.uk

Commonwealth War Graves Commission
2 Marlow Road
Maidenhead, Berkshire SL6 7DX
Phone: 01628 634221
www.cwgc.org

Corporation of London Record Office
PO Box 270, Guildhall
London EC2P 2EJ
Phone: 020 7332 1251
www.cityoflondon.gov.uk/leisure_heritag
e/libraries_archives_museums_galleries

For census returns from 1841-1891
(including the 1881 Census index)
The Family Records Centre
Myddelton Street
London EC1R 1UW
Phone: 020 8392 5300
www.open.gov.uk

General Register Office (Eire)
Joyce House
8-11 Lombard Street East
Dublin 2
www.groireland.ie

General Register Office (Northern Ireland)
Oxford House
49-55 Chichester Street
Belfast BT1 4HL
Phone: 028 90252000
www.nisra.gov.uk

General Register Office for Scotland
New Register House
Edinburgh EH1 3YT
Phone 0131 334 0380
www.gro-scotland.gov.uk

Huguenot Library
University College, Gower Street
London WC1E 6BT
www.ucl.ac.uk/library/huguenot.htm

Jewish Genealogical Society of Great
Britain
PO Box 13288
London N3 3WD
E-mail: jgsgb@ort.org

London Metropolitan Archives
40 Northampton Road
London EC1R OHB
Phone: 020 7332 3820
www.cityoflondon.gov.uk/archives/lma

National Archives of Ireland
Bishop Street
Dublin 8
Phone: 01 407 2300
www.nationalarchives.ie

National Library of Ireland
Kildare Street
Dublin 8
www.nli.ie

National Library of Wales
Penglais
Aberystwyth SY23 3BU
Phone: 01970 632800
www.llgc.org.uk

National Maritime Museum
Romney Road, Greenwich
London SE10 9NF
Phone: 020 8858 4422
www.nmm.ac.uk

National Monuments Record Centre
(England)
Great Western Village, Kemble Drive
Swindon, Wiltshire SN2 2GZ
Phone: 01793 414 600
www.english-heritage.org.uk

Ordnance Survey (Enquiries)
Romsey Road
Southampton SO16 4GU
Phone: 023 8079 2912
www.ordnancesurvey.co.uk

Parliamentary Archives
Record Office, House of Lords
London SW1A OPW
www.parliament.uk

Principal Registry of the Family Division
First Avenue House
42-49 High Holborn
London WCIV 6NP

Public Record Office
Ruskin Avenue
Kew
Surrey TW9 4DU
www.pro.gov.uk

Public Record Office of Northern Ireland
66 Balmoral Avenue
Belfast BT9 6NY
Phone: 028 9025 5905
www.proni.nics.gov.uk

Royal Commission on Historical
Manuscripts
Quality House, Quality Court
Chancery Lane
London WC2A 1HP
Phone: 020 7242 1198
www.hmc.gov.uk

Society of Friends' Library (Quakers)
Friends House
173-177 Euston Road
London NW1 2BJ
Phone: 020 7663 1135
www.quaker.org.uk

Society of Genealogists
14 Charterhouse Buildings
Goswell Road
London EC1M 7BA
Phone: 020 7251 8799
www.sog.org.uk

The British Library
96 Euston Road
London NW1 2DB
Phone: 020 7412 7513
www.bl.uk

The Church of Jesus Christ of Latter-day
Saints
399 Garretts Green Lane, Sheldon
Birmingham BB33 OUH
Phone: 0121 785 2200

The Federation of Family History Societies
PO Box 2425
Coventry CV5 6YX
Phone: 07041 492032 (mobile) - General
enquiries
Phone: 0161 797 3843 - Publications
www.ffhs.org.uk

The Guild of One Name Studies
c/o Box G, The Society of Genealogists
14 Charterhouse Buildings
Goswell Road
London ECIM 7BA
www.one-name.org

The Institute of Heraldic & Genealogical
Studies (IHGS)
79-82 Northgate
Canterbury
Kent CT1 1BA
Phone: 01227 768664
www.ihgs.ac.uk

The Office for National Statistics
The Family Records Centre
Myddelton Street
London EC1R 1UW
Phone: 0870 243 7788
www.open.gov.uk

York Probate Sub-Registry
Duncombe Place
York YO1 2EA
Phone: 01904 624210

Archival-Quality Materials

Conservation Resources (UK) Ltd.
Units 1, 2, 4 & 5 Pony Road
Horspath Industrial Estate
Cowley
Oxford OX4 2RD
Phone: 01865 747755

Secol Ltd.
Howlett Way
Thetford
Norfolk IP24 1HZ
Phone: 01842 752341

Silverprint
12 Valentine Place
London SE1 8QH
Phone: 020 7620 0844

Collage Workshops

Nicola.Maule@Virgin.net